✧ *Companions for the Journey* ✧

Praying with
Frédéric Ozanam

✧ *Companions for the Journey* ✧

Praying with
Frédéric Ozanam

by
Ronald Ramson, CM

Saint Mary's Press
Christian Brothers Publications
Winona, Minnesota

✧ To Frédéric and Vincent, ✧
thank you;
To the Vincentian Family,
thank you;
To my family,
thank you;
To my friends,
thank you.

Genuine recycled paper with 10% post-consumer waste.
Printed with soy-based ink.

The publishing team for this book included Carl Koch, series editor; Rosemary Broughton, development editor; Laurie A. Berg, copy editor; Alan S. Hanson, production editor and typesetter; Maurine R. Twait, art director; Elaine Kohner, illustrator; Kent Linder, cover designer; pre-press, printing, and binding by the graphics division of Saint Mary's Press.

The acknowledgments continue on page 120.

Printed in the United States of America

Printing: 9 8 7 6 5 4 3 2

Year: 2006 05 04 03 02 01 00 99 98

ISBN 0-88489-504-1

mLCm 2001/013 11 (B)

✦ Contents ✦

✧ Foreword ✧

Companions for the Journey

Just as food is required for human life, so are companions. Indeed, the word *companions* comes from two Latin words: *com,* meaning "with," and *panis,* meaning "bread." Companions nourish our heart, mind, soul, and body. They are also the people with whom we can celebrate the sharing of bread.

Perhaps the most touching stories in the Bible are about companionship: the Last Supper, the wedding feast at Cana, the sharing of the loaves and the fishes, and Jesus' breaking of bread with the disciples on the road to Emmaus. Each incident of companionship with Jesus revealed more about his mercy, love, wisdom, suffering, and hope. When Jesus went to pray in the Garden of Olives, he craved the companionship of the Apostles. They let him down. But God sent the Spirit to inflame the hearts of the Apostles, and they became faithful companions to Jesus and to one another.

Throughout history, other faithful companions have followed Jesus and the Apostles. These saints and mystics have also taken the journey from conversion, through suffering, to resurrection. Just as they were inspired by the holy people who went before them, so too may you be inspired by these saints and mystics and take them as your companions on your spiritual journey.

The Companions for the Journey series is a response to the spiritual hunger of Christians. This series makes available the rich spiritual teachings of mystics and guides whose wisdom can help us on our pilgrimage. As you complete the last meditation in each volume, it is hoped that you will feel supported, challenged, and affirmed by a soul-companion on your spiritual journey.

The spiritual hunger that has emerged over the last twenty years is a great sign of renewal in Christian life. People fill retreat programs and workshops on topics in spirituality. The demand for spiritual directors exceeds the number available. Interest in the lives and writings of saints and mystics is increasing as people search for models of whole and holy Christian life.

Praying with Frédéric

Praying with Frédéric Ozanam is more than just a book about Frédéric's spirituality. This book seeks to engage you in praying in the way that Frédéric did about issues and themes that were central to his experience. Each meditation can enlighten your understanding of his spirituality and lead you to reflect on your own experience.

The goal of *Praying with Frédéric Ozanam* is that you will discover Frédéric's rich spirituality and integrate his spirit and wisdom into your relationship with God, with your brothers and sisters, and with your own heart and mind.

Suggestions for Praying with Frédéric

Meet Frédéric Ozanam, a fascinating companion for your pilgrimage, by reading the introduction to this book. It provides a brief biography of Frédéric and an outline of the major themes of his spirituality.

Once you meet Frédéric Ozanam, you will be ready to pray with him and to encounter God, your sisters and brothers, and yourself in new and wonderful ways. To help your prayer, here are some suggestions that have been part of the tradition of Christian spirituality:

Create a sacred space. Jesus said, "'Whenever you pray, go into your room and shut the door and pray to your [God] who is in secret; and your [God] who sees in secret will reward you'" (Matthew 6:6). Solitary prayer is best done in a place where you can have privacy and silence, both of which can be luxuries in the life of busy people. If privacy and silence are not possible, create a quiet, safe place within yourself, perhaps while riding to and from work, while sitting in line at the dentist's office, or while waiting for someone. Do the best you can, knowing that a loving God is present everywhere. Whether the meditations in this book are used for solitary prayer or with a group, try to create a prayerful mood with candles, meditative music, an open Bible, or a crucifix.

Open yourself to the power of prayer. Every human experience has a religious dimension. All of life is suffused with God's presence. So remind yourself that God is present as you begin your period of prayer. Do not worry about distractions. If something keeps intruding during your prayer, spend some time talking with God about it. Be flexible because God's spirit blows where it will.

Prayer can open your mind and widen your vision. Be open to new ways of seeing God, people, and yourself. As you open yourself to the spirit of God, different emotions are evoked, such as sadness from tender memories, or joy from a celebration recalled. Our emotions are messages from God that can tell us much about our spiritual quest. Also, prayer strengthens our will to act. Through prayer, God can touch our will and empower us to live according to what we know is true.

Finally, many of the meditations in this book will call you to employ your memories, your imagination, and the circumstances of your life as subjects for prayer. The great mystics and saints realized that they had to use all their resources to know God better. Indeed, God speaks to us continually and touches us constantly. We must learn to listen and feel with all the means that God has given us.

Come to prayer with an open mind, heart, and will.

Preview each meditation before beginning. After you have placed yourself in God's presence, spend a few moments previewing the readings and especially the reflection activities. Several reflection activities are given in each meditation because different styles of prayer appeal to different personalities or personal needs. **Note that each meditation has more reflection activities than can be done during one prayer period.**

Therefore, select only one or two reflection activities each time you use a meditation. Do not feel compelled to complete all the reflection activities.

Read meditatively. Each meditation offers you a story about Frédéric and a reading from his writings. Take your time reading. If a particular phrase touches you, stay with it. Relish its feelings, meanings, and concerns.

Use the reflections. Following the readings is a short reflection in commentary form, which is meant to give perspective to the readings. Then you are offered several ways of meditating on the readings and the theme of the prayer. You may be familiar with the different methods of meditating, but in case you are not, they are described briefly here:

✦ *Repeated short prayer or mantra:* One means of focusing your prayer is to use a *mantra,* or "prayer word." The mantra may be a single word or a short phrase taken from the readings or from the Scriptures. For example, a short prayer for meditation 2 in this book might simply be "Rejoice in the Lord always." Repeated slowly in harmony with your breathing, the mantra helps you center your heart and mind on one action or attribute of God.

✦ *Lectio divina:* This type of meditation is "divine studying," a concentrated reflection on the word of God or the wisdom of a spiritual writer. Most often in *lectio divina,* you will be invited to read one of the passages several times and then concentrate on one or two sentences, pondering their meaning for you and their effect on you. *Lectio divina* commonly ends with formulation of a resolution.

✦ *Guided meditation:* In this type of meditation, our imagination helps us consider alternative actions and likely consequences. Our imagination helps us experience new ways of seeing God, our neighbors, ourselves, and nature. When Jesus told his followers parables and stories, he engaged their imagination. In this book, you will be invited to follow guided meditations.

One way of doing a guided meditation is to read the scene or story several times, until you know the outline and can recall it when you enter into reflection. Or before your prayer time, you may wish to record the meditation on a tape recorder. If so, remember to allow pauses for reflection between phrases and to speak with a slow, peaceful pace and tone. Then, during prayer, when you have finished the readings and the reflection commentary, you can turn on your recording of the meditation and be led through it. If you find your own voice too distracting, ask a friend to make the tape for you.

✦ *Examen of consciousness:* The reflections often will ask you to examine how God has been speaking to you in your past and present experience—in other words, the reflections will ask you to examine your awareness of God's presence in your life.

✦ *Journal writing:* Writing is a process of discovery. If you write for any length of time, stating honestly what is on your mind and in your heart, you will unearth much about who you are, how you stand with your God, what deep longings reside in your soul, and more. In some reflections, you will be asked to write a dialog with Jesus or someone else. If you have never used writing as a means of meditation, try it. Reserve a special notebook for your journal writing. If desired, you can go back to your entries at a future time for an examen of consciousness.

✦ *Action:* Occasionally, a reflection will suggest singing a favorite hymn, going out for a walk, or undertaking some other physical activity. Actions can be meaningful forms of prayer.

Using the Meditations for Group Prayer

If you wish to use the meditations for community prayer, these suggestions may help:

✦ Read the theme to the group. Call the community into the presence of God, using the short opening prayer. Invite one or two participants to read one or both readings. If you use both readings, observe the pause between them.

✦ The reflection commentary may be used as a reading, or it can be deleted, depending on the needs and interests of the group.

✦ Select one of the reflection activities for your group. Allow sufficient time for your group to reflect, to recite a centering prayer or mantra, to accomplish a studying prayer (*lectio divina*), or to finish an examen of consciousness. Depending on the group and the amount of available time, you may want to invite the participants to share their reflections, responses, or petitions with the group.

✦ Reading the passage from the Scriptures may serve as a summary of the meditation.

✦ If a formulated prayer or a psalm is given as a closing, it may be recited by the entire group. Or you may ask participants to offer their own prayers for the closing.

Now you are ready to begin praying with Frédéric Ozanam, a faithful and caring companion on this stage of your spiritual journey. It is hoped that you will find him to be a true soul-companion.

CARL KOCH
Editor

✧ Introduction ✧

Many will praise his understanding;
   it will never be blotted out.
His memory will not disappear,
   and his name will live through all generations.
Nations will speak of his wisdom,
   and the congregation will proclaim his praise.

(Sirach 39:9–10)

These words of sacred Scripture grace the tomb of Frédéric Ozanam, which is located in the crypt of the Church of Saint-Joseph-des-Carmes, adjacent to the famous Institut Catholique in Paris.

They are appropriate words for a man whose memory has lived in the mind and heart of countless individuals since his death in 1853. Many have praised his understanding in the areas of literature and history. People from all nations do recount his wisdom.

Frédéric Ozanam was one of the most celebrated professors at the Sorbonne, the University of Paris, where a lecture hall has been dedicated to his memory. His doctoral dissertation, *Dante and Catholic Philosophy in the Thirteenth Century,* helped direct scholarly thinking on the master Italian poet. Frédéric received the prestigious Gobert Prize from the French Academy for his major work *History of Civilization in the Fifth Century,* a work recognized as having the "'highest literary merit'" (Louis Baunard, *Ozanam in His Correspondence,* p. 410). Frédéric's masterpiece, *The Franciscan Poets of Italy in the Thirteenth Century,* has been acclaimed as an indispensable authority on the history of literature, on Catholicism, and on Italy. During his lifetime Frédéric was elected to membership in the renowned Academies of Florence, Rome, Bavaria, and Lyon, a true mark of the professional esteem with which he was regarded.

As great as all these academic accomplishments are, Frédéric's memory has continued to live on throughout the generations mainly because of a nonacademic achievement: the founding of the Society of Saint Vincent de Paul. People of every continent, culture, status, and race have joined this association of charity to put into action the dual commandment of love for God and for our neighbor mandated by Jesus. This love should manifest itself in works of mercy according to the example of its founder, Frédéric Ozanam.

Pope John Paul II has referred to Frédéric Ozanam as a gift to the church:

> We must thank God for the present he has made to the Church, in the person of Ozanam. One never ceases to wonder at the amount of work he was able to undertake for the Church, for the community, for the poor. (27 April 1983)

No one is ever canonized a saint in the Catholic church because of achievements. A man or woman is canonized because he or she has lived a life of heroic virtue. When Frédéric Ozanam is declared a saint, it will be because he lived in fidelity to God's grace and he practiced virtue to a heroic degree as a Catholic layman—a husband and father, a writer and professor, a founder and a member of the Society of Saint Vincent de Paul. The church has, in fact, officially testified to the heroic sanctity of Frédéric Ozanam when, on 6 July 1993, Pope John Paul II published the decree stating the heroicity of virtues of Frédéric. On 25 June 1996, the same pope signed the decree for Frédéric's beatification that took place in Paris during World Youth Days on 22 August 1997.

This gift to the people of God, Frédéric Ozanam, is then someone every Christian can admire and emulate. Not everyone may be able to duplicate his intellectual prowess and literary masterpieces, but everyone can imitate his holiness of life and compassionate service to others. In a world that has few genuine and authentic heroes, in a world where the integrity and credibility of people is often questioned and seen with skepticism, Frédéric Ozanam stands tall as a generous and committed friend, a model and example, indeed a gift to today's church and world. He is an ideal Christian layman for the third millennium.

Frédéric's Story

France

Victor Hugo in his epic of 1862, *Les Miserables,* portrayed nineteenth-century France with accuracy and clarity. The country was reeling from the aftershocks of revolution and the Napoleonic wars, which occurred in the time frame from 1789 to 1815. Society was in the throes of radical political and social change, catapulting in its governmental structure from a monarchy to a republic to an empire, then changing from an empire to a monarchy and to an empire once again, and finally moving to a second republic. While this was happening politically, the industrial revolution had also affected the social and economic spheres. The rich grew richer due to preferential treatment by the government and due to the greed that obsessed them. Pauperism was rampant; unemployment and homelessness were epidemic; the poor lived from hand to mouth. Men, women, and children worked long hours under inhuman conditions for unjust wages. Certain members of the privileged class, including Victor Hugo, would advocate social reform, but their efforts bore little fruit. Few of the upper class wanted to get their hands dirty assisting *les miserables* in their foul and filthy slums; few of the rich wanted to risk change in the operations of industry.

The nonreligious Napoleon reopened the churches closed by the revolution, but things were not the same religiously as they had been. Indifference and hostility toward Christianity mushroomed. The church was singled out as a major scapegoat for the social, political, and economic unrest. Anticlericalism reigned. In the estimation of many, the altar and the throne were still too closely associated, although Catholicism was in fact no longer the religion of the state. Strong traces of Jansenism infiltrated the spiritual life of the faithful who braved turmoil and upheaval. This spirituality mitigated against many Christians getting overly involved in the affairs of the day. Frédéric Ozanam's life as a French Catholic who was actively engaged in the affairs of the world and who pursued truth with joy stands out more boldly in this context of disaffection, national turmoil, and rapid change.

Who Was Frédéric Ozanam?

Antoine Frédéric Ozanam was born 23 April 1813, in the city of Milan, Italy, then under the French governance of Napoleon. His father, Jean-Antoine-François Ozanam, a native of Chalamont, France, retired from the army with the rank of captain at the age of twenty-five because he had been severely wounded during Napoleon's Italian campaign. Jean-Antoine was a man of fierce patriotism, honor, and courage who became a medical doctor of local renown. Napoleon decorated Dr. Ozanam with the Iron Crown in appreciation of his extraordinary service at the Milan Military Hospital during a typhus fever epidemic.

Frédéric's mother was Marie Nantes, the daughter of a successful silk merchant of Lyon. As a child, she could remember the horrors of the siege of Lyon in 1793, when two thousand people were executed. She and her sisters had to hide and live in cellars. She could remember her teenage brother being shot to death; her parents and family only escaped death by fleeing to Switzerland with the assistance of an old uncle, a Carthusian priest.

Frédéric Ozanam was the fifth child of a family of fourteen, eleven of whom died in infancy or youth. In addition to Frédéric, his family included his parents, his sister Elisa, and his brother Alphonse. His brother Charles was born later. Living with the family was the beloved Marie Gruziat, whom the children called "Guigui"; she was cook, housekeeper, and nanny. Guigui served four generations of Ozanams and was always regarded as one of the family. Members of the family consulted her on important matters in their life.

The family traced the Ozanam name back to a seventh-century Jew, Samuel Hosannam. Samuel was converted by Saint Didier, the bishop of Vienna, whom Samuel and his family had sheltered from the persecution of Queen Brunhilde.

The queen eventually had Didier assassinated because he reproved her immoral behavior. Interestingly, the Didier name has remained among the Ozanam descendants.

Frédéric was baptized 13 May 1813 in the Servite church of Saint Mary's, which is now dedicated to the great cardinal archbishop of Milan, Saint Charles Borromeo.

When the city of Milan was ceded to the Austrians through a treaty in 1815, Frédéric's father decided to relocate the family to Lyon, the birthplace and home of his wife, Marie. The patriot Dr. Ozanam refused to live in or raise his family in a city under foreign control. Lyon became the city where Frédéric grew up and received his primary education. He always looked upon himself as a Lyonnaise.

Elisa, together with her mother, taught Frédéric how to read and write. Even though Elisa was twelve years his senior, this brother and sister grew remarkably close. Frédéric was a product of home schooling until his parents judged him ready for the Academy of Lyon in 1822. Frédéric showed exceptional intellectual ability early in life and a high energy level for work. His Achilles' heel, however, was his health. At seven years old, Frédéric almost died from typhoid fever. His parents never left his side for fifteen days and nights. In his delirium, Frédéric asked for a beer, and the beer cured him (so he

writes!). His parents held a different version of his cure. They believed that Frédéric's recovery was due to the intercession of Saint John Francis Regis, the French Jesuit saint who was a favorite of theirs because of his dedication to the poor and the underprivileged. Frédéric's mother and father prayed persistently to the saint for his intercession, even pinning a relic of Saint John Francis to Frédéric's pajamas. In their minds, their son was cured miraculously.

Six months after Frédéric's recovery, his beloved teenage sister, Elisa, died. It was a time of great sorrow for the family, especially for Frédéric. He suffered intense pain at the loss of his "first teacher."

Frédéric the Teenager

Frédéric's close friend and mentor, Fr. Joseph Noirot, gives an in-depth description of Frédéric at this time of his life.

> "Nature had marvellously endowed him with intelligence and a good heart. Affectionate and loving, devoted, modest, sympathetic, passionate and keen, playful yet serious, hating nobody, but having no patience with liars. Never was there a student more popular with his classsmates. In the words of one of them, they surrounded him with affection and almost respect." (Madeleine des Rivières, *Ozanam*, p. 29)

When he was thirteen years old, Frédéric began writing prose and poetry in Latin and in French. A gift to his parents was a small collection of these compositions. He wrote the dedication to his father in Latin, but out of thoughtful consideration for his mother, he translated it into French.

Frédéric started the study of philosophy in 1829; he was sixteen years old. This proved to be the time in his life when he experienced severe doubts about his faith. This crisis lasted for almost a year. The crisis finally ceased after Frédéric committed his life to the service of truth. Lengthy conversations with one of his professors of philosophy, Fr. Joseph Noirot, helped Frédéric reach further intellectual clarity. Frédéric never again would experience doubts about his faith, and until the day he died, Frédéric was accused of excessive gentleness toward those people who did experience doubts or who classified themselves as unbelievers. He remembered the pain.

By age seventeen, Frédéric had become fluent in Latin and Greek. He enjoyed speaking to his father in Latin. Later, he would learn German, Hebrew, English, and Sanskrit, the sacred language of India.

While he was still a teenager, Frédéric wrote two articles in the *Precurseur*, a newspaper of Lyon, refuting the doctrine of Saint-Simon. The newspaper had been praising the new "replacement" for Christianity. Although Frédéric was well aware of his youth and inexperience as a journalist, his passion for truth and his love for the church impelled him to write the articles.

The articles were expanded to booklet form in the spring of 1831 under the title *Reflections on the Doctrine of Saint-Simon*. The work was immediately acclaimed for its clarity and precision, two qualities that would become hallmarks of Frédéric's writings. Readers of the articles and booklet looked forward to future works by an even more mature and experienced author.

Frédéric and Paris

In 1831, the eighteen-year-old Frédéric moved to Paris, a city that was then dirty, gloomy, and overpopulated. The Paris that the world knows today as the City of Lights did not appear until the 1850s, under the reign of Napoleon III. In deference to the wishes of his father, Frédéric enrolled in the school of law. Dr. Ozanam's dream was that his son would one day hold a position on the royal court of justice. Law was not Frédéric's preference; his heart's desires were literature and history. He would fulfill those desires later.

While studying at the Sorbonne, Frédéric met both friend and foe. He became acquainted with the shining lights of nineteenth-century French Catholicism: Chateaubriand, Lamartine, Montalembert, Ampère, Lacordaire, Gerbet, and others. At the same time, in the lecture halls and corridors of the university, Frédéric heard and felt the attacks of anti-Catholicism and anticlericalism. These were voiced by professors and savants who enjoyed the sport of scorning the church and ridiculing those students whom they suspected of being practicing Catholics. In a short time, Frédéric gathered a small group of students with similar feelings and convictions as himself, young men of an ardent and living faith. Their corporate unity and courage helped them to counter hostile attacks against the truth of the faith. Two of their prime opponents were Marc Girardin, professor of history, who had attacked the papacy and the clergy; and Theodore Jouffroy, who held the chair of philosophy. Jouffroy's course was their battlefield because he attacked Divine Revelation and refuted even the possibility of such. The young Catholic students' persistence resulted in retractions by both professors.

The Conference of History

Frédéric collaborated with Emmanuel Bailly, editor of the *Catholic Tribune*, in forming the Conference of History, which met every Saturday. The two built this association on the remnants of the Society of Good Studies, an organization which Bailly had previously founded but had disbanded after the July 1830 revolution. The conference consisted of Catholic and non-Catholic members who discussed a variety of subjects: history, geography, art, philosophy, literature, and economics—but not politics.

At a particular meeting in the spring of 1833, Frédéric and the others were challenged by a proponent of Saint-Simonism. This movement, intended to be a replacement for Christianity, was generated by Claude Henri, Count Saint-Simon, who had died eight years earlier but whose theories were still being advocated. Saint-Simonism declared that doctrines and creeds were unimportant and that society moved strictly by social and economic forces. Saint-Simon challenged Christianity to establish a more equitable and just social order. It was logical, therefore, that this peer criticized Frédéric and the other members of the conference for doing little or nothing to alleviate the needs of the suffering poor or to promote social justice in the church and society.

Frédéric knew in his heart that his challenger was right. In spite of the good done socially and academically for members of the Conference of History, Frédéric said that "'one thing is wanting . . . works of charity. The blessing of the poor is the blessing of God'" (Baunard, *Correspondence*, p. 65). Frédéric and several friends decided to meet the following week to see what they might do.

The Society of Saint Vincent de Paul

On the evening of 23 April 1833, Frédéric's twentieth birthday, six students—Augustine Le Taillandier, François Lallier, Felix Clave, Jules Devaux, Paul Lamache, Frédéric Ozanam—and their mentor, Emmanuel Bailly, met in the offices of the *Catholic Tribune*. On that night the Conference of Charity was born. Frédéric Ozanam was the primary founder, inspiration, and soul of the Conference. In 1835, with the formulation of the first rules, the name of the Conference was officially changed to the Society of Saint Vincent de Paul, a name that they had begun to adopt the previous year.

The small group of seven added an eighth member; then they expanded to fifteen. Amazingly, the conference began to mushroom. During the first five years, membership increased to more than two thousand in fifteen centers throughout France. Although the Society was still composed principally of students, by 1838 others had joined the Society. Several of these were men in high places. Most of the expansion of the Society took place when students would return home from school and encourage others to join them in establishing local Conferences of the Society. The Society took fire from the spark within its membership.

Members of the Society refer to their individual groups as conferences and to themselves as Vincentians. From the beginning the key to their ministry to the poor and needy was home visitation. Members would always go in pairs to the homes of the poor after the exhortation of Jesus who sent his Apostles and disciples two by two to continue his mission.

No form of charity was foreign to the Society. Not only did Frédéric and the others take care of the physical and material needs of others (food, shelter, clothing, firewood), they also involved themselves with tutoring, even setting up libraries for members of the military. During the bloody revolutionary skirmishes, Vincentians attended to the wounded and the dying. In every work, members of the Society were solicitous to the spiritual and moral welfare of others.

Frédéric insisted that Vincentians not restrict their charity to Catholics, but be the servants of all those in need. He also proposed that countries help one another, especially in situations of national catastrophes. This insistence on mutuality may well be traced back to Frédéric's early involvement with the Society for the Propagation of the Faith in Lyon and its missionary outreach. Frédéric supported the Society of Paris when they aided the Society in Dublin during the Irish famine (1845–1850). Dublin reciprocated during the horrible revolution of 1848 in France.

On 30 January 1853, Frédéric reported at a meeting in Florence, Italy, that the Society included two thousand members in Paris alone, where they were visiting approximately one-third of all the poor in that city. Membership numbered five hundred separate conferences throughout France and was continuing to spread across the whole of Europe and onto other continents. During Frédéric's lifetime he witnessed the establishment of the Society in Italy, Belgium, Scotland, Ireland, England, Germany, the United States, Holland, Greece, Turkey, Jerusalem, Switzerland, Austria, Mexico, and Canada.

Conferences of Notre Dame

While he was a student in Paris, Frédéric approached the Parisian archbishop, De Quelen, with a petition signed by a number of fellow students. It asked him to allow Fr. Henri Lacordaire to preach a series of talks or conferences in Notre Dame Cathedral. Father Lacordaire had generated a name for himself in the classroom and in the pulpit at Stanislas College of Paris. Frédéric wanted someone dynamic and brilliant who could present the Gospel in a way that counteracted the atheistic social doctrine that was slowly but surely dragging the nation into materialism.

Archbishop de Quelen received Frédéric's occasional petitions but did not respond for almost three years—at least not in the way that Frédéric and his peers wanted. But the prelate finally acceded to Frédéric's requests, perhaps because of Frédéric's prudent and respectful persistence, reminiscent of the person who kept banging at the neighbor's door in the Gospel of Luke (cf. Luke 11:5–8).

Frédéric was asked by the editor of a leading Catholic newspaper of Paris to act as official reporter for the conferences. He and several Vincentians handled the publicity for the series. And the people came! Over five thousand persons, students and intellectuals, packed Notre Dame to hear the young Dominican priest preach. In attendance were such famous people as Chateaubriand, Victor Hugo, Ampère, Tocqueville, Balzac, Dumas, Montalembert, and Victor Cousins. Archbishop de Quelen and his canons sat directly in front of the pulpit.

Lacordaire ascended the pulpit of the great cathedral and captured his audience with his eloquence and delivery. He explained how religious truth was related to social truth, and he showed how religious truth was united to freedom, equality, and fraternity, the three key words of the French Revolution. Lacordaire had abandoned the traditional style of preaching and delivered his message with current examples and historical comparisons comprehensible to everyone present.

At his conclusion the audience burst into applause. Lacordaire had exceeded everyone's expectations. The archbishop was overjoyed and expressed his gratitude to God. The crowds packed Notre Dame during the remaining Sundays of Lent. Lacordaire would continue to preach the Lenten conferences through the years until 1850.

No one could forget that the establishment of the Conferences of Notre Dame was due to Frédéric Ozanam's persistence and his faith in the person of Lacordaire. But behind that was his passion for truth, which fueled the persistence. Lacordaire and Frédéric would remain close friends throughout their lives. Lacordaire was one of Frédéric's earliest biographers.

The Propagation of the Faith

While in Lyon, Frédéric Ozanam had become involved with the Society for the Propagation of the Faith. A fellow parishioner of Saint Nizier's in Lyon, the teenager Pauline Marie Jaricot, founded an association to help support the French foreign missions through the distribution of alms and the intercessory prayers of the faithful. The French Revolution had wiped out the missionary agencies. Jaricot wanted to establish one association to help Catholic missionaries everywhere.

In 1822, the vicar general of New Orleans, Fr. Angelo Inglesi, came to raise funds for Bishop Louis Dubourg's missions in the United States. Father Inglesi gathered a group of twelve laypeople into an association to support his endeavors. Jaricot's organization was so well structured that Inglesi's association joined hers to form the Society for the Propagation of the Faith on 3 May 1822. From the society's beginning, financial aid was sent to the missions in China, Asia, Africa, and the United States.

Frédéric had the soul of a missionary. One of his dreams was to be an apostle and a martyr. Because of his love for the church and its missionary efforts, Frédéric remained actively involved in the Society for the Propagation of the Faith. He edited the society's annals for almost ten years and acted as a liaison between its Paris and Lyon councils.

The Scholar

Frédéric obtained his doctorate of law degree in 1836, at the age of twenty-three. Three years later he received his doctorate of literature, the fulfillment of his heart's desire.

In 1841, Frédéric began to teach at the Sorbonne as well as at the secondary school, the Stanislas College in Paris. At the university he first taught as a replacement for the invalid M. Fauriel in the position of assistant professor in the chair of foreign literature.

The chair to which Ozanam was named was one which his mental and moral endowments fitted him admirably to fill. It was the realization, moreover, of those ambitions which he had cherished, like the presentiment of a mission, and for whose fulfilment he had been preparing himself from his early boyhood. (Kathleen O'Meara, *Frédéric Ozanam: His Life and Works*, p. 147)

It was in the classroom as a professor of literature where Frédéric's genius shone. His courses were the talk of the Sorbonne. His teaching ability, his brilliantly developed and delivered lectures, his originality of thought, and his orthodoxy of faith attracted overflowing numbers to his lecture hall. Later, after his marriage and some anxious times, Frédéric was appointed in 1844 to full professor at the Sorbonne.

Marriage

For some time Frédéric had thought of a vocation to the priesthood in the Dominican order, but he came to understand that it was God's will that he serve God and the church as a layman.

In the midst of his vastly active ministry to the poor, his teaching obligations, and numerous publications, Frédéric met a young woman, Amélie Soulacroix, through the matchmaking efforts of his priest friend, Fr. Joseph Noirot. Frédéric and Amélie were married in Lyon at the church of Saint Nizier on 23 June 1841. Fr. Alphonse Ozanam witnessed the marriage, and Frédéric's other brother, Dr. Charles Ozanam, served the wedding mass. Frédéric was twenty-eight years old; Amélie was nineteen. After four years and two miscarriages, Amélie gave birth to a daughter, Marie, their only child, named after Frédéric's mother and the Blessed Virgin Mary.

The Newspaper

In 1848, with the help of some friends who shared his thinking, Frédéric founded a Catholic newspaper, the *New Era*. It did intend to espouse any political party, so that it could print the truth with impartiality, moderation, and charity. Frédéric promoted social justice for the poor and the working class. He also defended the founding of a Christian political party that trusted in the Second French Republic. The first edition of the newspaper appeared on the fifteenth of April. It had 1,100 subscribers, and in two month's time, it grew to 3,200 subscribers.

The spring and early summer of 1848 were highly volatile times in Paris. Frédéric and the other journalists urged the clergy and Catholics in the public sector to recognize the hand of providence in the revolutionary process and to cooperate with whatever legal form of government emerged. Citizens were urged to respect civil order, but civil order was not to be. Angry mobs of citizens stormed the National Assembly. Toward the end of June, widespread uprisings led to a state of emergency; the military reacted quickly, and bloody bouts ensued in combat with the insurgent citizens. By the end of the month, the Second Republic had died. And so did the newspaper.

Frédéric's Final Days

Frédéric devoted much of the last five years of his life to ministering to the poor and to guiding the rapidly expanding Society of Saint Vincent de Paul.

Overextension in activity coupled with inner intensity, each fueled by the fire of zeal, caught up with Frédéric and wreaked havoc on his fragile health. Doctors insisted that Frédéric cease all activity and get some rest. With the desire that his health return, Amélie took Frédéric and their daughter to the Tuscany area of Italy in the hope that the warm weather would revitalize him.

After months of ups and downs, Frédéric grew weaker. Kidney pain and edema were increasing. He prayed for the grace to die in his beloved France. Against the better judgment of his physicians, on the last day of August, Amélie booked passage on a ship to France; she was taking her dying husband home. He died shortly after their arrival in the port city of Marseilles on 8 September 1853. Frédéric was forty years old. The speculation was that Frédéric had died of tuberculosis. It is now believed, however, that his illness was Bright's disease, originating from tuberculosis.

Frédéric's beloved wife, Amélie, wanted him buried in Paris at Saint-Joseph-des-Carmes. Frédéric's longtime friend Father Lacordaire, now provincial of the Dominicans, arranged for Frédéric's body to be buried in the crypt of the church alongside the priests martyred during the 1792 massacres. It seemed appropriate that he rest beside those who shed their blood for the faith, having given, day by day and year by year, his own life for the enduring faith of the church.

Praying with Frédéric Ozanam

Frédéric was a man of passion—love for his faith, zeal for the truth, and ardency in compassion. If someone were to design his coat of arms, those three words could well serve as Frédéric's motto and appear on the ribbon scroll under the emblem: Faith, Truth, Compassion.

Faith

Faith was the sacred fire for Frédéric. It was both a virtue to be nourished and a gift to be shared. It was a grace and a heritage in his life that made him justifiably proud and insistent in its public proclamation. Faith gave him the nobility and the call to serve the poor with intelligence, humility, and mercy. Frédéric understood the importance of Christians to be, and to be seen as, apostles sent to counteract the coldness of the world by the ardent fire of faith. He saw the importance of fraternal support in practicing the works of mercy. Above all, he saw Christ in the persons of the poor, and he responded to them as the representatives of his master.

Truth

While he was still young, Frédéric stated that his mission in life was the service of truth. Falsehood and half-truths were to be shunned. Truth needed to be uncovered, articulated, and publicized. Frédéric, in his passion for truth, could not tolerate duplicity and hypocrisy. Ignorance was always an enemy to be overcome. Seeking wisdom and truth was an attractive and satisfying endeavor. Truth did indeed set one free. It brought light and joy to the intellect and peace to the soul.

Compassion

Frédéric's manner, though intense and ever-active, was always cordial and friendly—even gentle. He learned from his own difficulties and doubts to be patient with others in their turmoil. He enjoyed being with others: those who were older like his parents, Father Noirot, M. Ampère, M. Bailly; his peers, Lallier, Lacordaire, Amélie; and the young, his students and his daughter. But his compassion was shown most strongly in his love for poor people. He gave them time, sympathy, and respect. His writings show his empathy with their often frightful circumstances, his capacity for mutuality, his honor toward them in their suffering. Frédéric lived the dual commandment to love God and to love one's neighbor as oneself.

Frédéric for Today

Like Frédéric, we experience a fragmented world, a world of turmoil, confusion, injustice, poverty, and insensitivity to others. Frédéric cultivated in himself and in others the virtues that were remedies or antidotes to these.

Frédéric knew the meaning of fragile health and suffering, and he learned patience and gratitude as he became reconciled with these. He was also a talented man who responded to the gifts he had been given. He brought his abilities and capacities to his relationships within his family, to his scholarly work as a professor, and to his service of the poor. Frédéric was able to see Christ in the person of the poor, the sick, and the abandoned. The poor were, in a felt sense, his own—his children, his brothers and sisters, his Lord and Savior, his master.

Who can appreciate Frédéric today? Laity in the church will find a kindred spirit in Frédéric Ozanam, be they single people or married couples, students or teachers, working professionals or active volunteers. Clergy in the church will find a collaborating spirit in Frédéric Ozanam, be they vowed in community or serving in diocesan positions.

Persons who desire a well-integrated Christian as their patron will find in Frédéric a man in whom intelligence and affectivity met and embraced, a man who lived his familial life, professional life, and life of charitable service to the poor in a balanced way.

Believers who are undergoing major life transitions can find an exemplar in Frédéric Ozanam, whether the transition is from single life to marriage, from student life to post-graduation challenges, from the identity of a young professional to that of an acknowledged authority, from a life of vibrant health to a time of convalescence.

Adults in nurturing or authoritative positions will find a model in Frédéric Ozanam. Along with being a husband and father, he became an authentic father figure to students, a peer to his colleagues, and an inspiring founder and coordinator for the members of the Society of Saint Vincent de Paul. Frédéric was able to appreciate his heritage as well as to take the initiative in dealing with the problems of his present. He kept his eye on the future and was committed to the advancement of civilization and the well-being of humans in the ever changing social order.

Inheriting a Compassionate Heart

Theme: Parental love and example, given in God's love, endure for a lifetime.

Opening prayer: Compassionate God, thank you for loving parents and the example they give me over the years.

About Frédéric

The Ozanams, Frédéric's parents, learned much from the school of life: the horrors of revolution, the ravages of war, the vulnerability of bankruptcy, the death of one child after another, the necessity of relocation, and the pursuit of several careers. Yet through these experiences, their Christian faith endured.

Frédéric described his father, Dr. Jean-Antoine-François Ozanam, as a man of

> "an ardent faith, a noble character, [with] a high regard for justice, a tireless charity towards the poor. He loved science, art and work. He inspired us with a taste for the beautiful and the sublime." (Baunard, *Correspondence*, p. 3)

Frédéric also spoke in glowing terms of his mother, Marie Ozanam. He credits her with teaching him the faith in word and action. Frédéric refers to her as "saintly." He writes: "'It is at her knees that I learned to fear You, O Lord! and from her looks to love You'" (Baunard, *Correspondence*, p. 7).

Frédéric learned compassion, the key to his own spirituality, from his parents' compassion shown to the sick poor. Dr. Ozanam often attended the sick in their homes. After attending to their medical needs, he knelt at their bedside praying to the divine physician for their recovery and healing. Upon reviewing his father's estate and his business affairs following his death, Frédéric remarked:

> "I owe him this tribute, . . . that I was able to show with the figures before me, that one-third of his professional visits were made to known poor without any hope whatever of fees." (Baunard, *Correspondence*, p. 137)

The example he gave Frédéric was matched by the paternal encouragement in Frédéric's own endeavors. Eight days after the elder Ozanam's death, Frédéric reminisced:

> My father knew from its beginning and loved our Society of Saint Vincent de Paul. He rejoiced to see his son called as one of the first to take part in it. He often encouraged by his advice and example my inexperience in good works. He himself always welcomed and assisted the poor, whose unanimous sympathy is today one of our comforts. (Joseph I. Dirvin, trans. and ed., *Frédéric Ozanam: A Life in Letters*, p. 111)

Frédéric's mother, too, was actively involved in work beyond her domestic circle. She presided for years over an association of women called the Night Watchers. The purpose of this organization was to minister to the infirm poor during the night. In later years she, as well as her husband, would climb to the top floors of the tenements in Lyon to care for the sick poor. In fact, it was an accident in one of the tenements that precipitated the doctor's death.

At his mother's death, two years after that of his father, Frédéric discovered among her papers notes that she used for the religious instruction of poor children and adults. A now-orphaned Frédéric prayed:

"May I . . . continue in thought, in faith, and in virtue, that communion with them which nothing was able to interrupt, and may their death not make any other change in our family than the addition to it of two saints." (Baunard, *Correspondence*, p. 157)

Frédéric had the example of twenty years of compassionate love for the sick poor before his eyes in the persons of his parents. This modeling cannot be underestimated as an inheritance brought to bear in the future ministry of the Society of Saint Vincent de Paul and in Frédéric's devotion to all those for whom he was responsible. Like parents, like son.

Pause: Can you recall situations in which your parents showed compassionate concern for those outside the family circle?

Frédéric's Words

[God's love] causes one to love his parents . . . because their lessons have conducted us in the right path and their affection kept us there. (Dirvin, trans. and ed., *Letters*, p. 36)
    I am filled with thanks to God for having brought me into the world in one of those situations on the border of hardship and of ease, which is used to privations without permitting enjoyment to be completely unknown, where one can go to bed with all his wants assuaged, but where one is no longer distraught by the continual clamors of necessity. God knows, with the natural weakness of my character, what dangers the softness of the wealthy or the abjection of the indigent classes would pose for me. I also feel that this humble position in which I am at present has brought me to serve like persons better. (Dirvin, trans. and ed., *Letters*, p. 91)

Reflection

During his entire life, Frédéric Ozanam exhibited a pride in his church and in his parents. He wrote:

> "Being a Christian, I glory in belonging to no other school than that of Truth, which is the Church. . . . I live by my faith which I have from my God, and by my honour which I have from my parents. You will allow me to defend the one and the other." (Baunard, *Correspondence*, p. 63)

For Frédéric, it was not only the love of his parents that brought him to the love of God, but also, as he later understood it, the love of God that gave him an enduring affection and esteem for his parents.

Frédéric invites us to reflect on parental love, our family background, the examples of concern that our parents exemplified for us outside the family circle, the gifts we have inherited from them, and the new things we learn about them after their death.

✧ In preparation for this meditation, have at hand four small sheets of paper, a journal, a pen, and a candle. Light the candle and sit quietly for ten minutes. Pray for the Spirit to enlighten you. Reflect on four qualities you have inherited from your parents that are also Christian virtues, qualities that belong to the life of the church. Write one quality on each of the four small sheets of paper.

+ First, arrange the qualities written on your four sheets of paper in their order of importance to you in your relationship to God. Write this series in your journal.
+ Then, arrange these qualities in the order of their importance to the members of your family or immediate community. Write these also in your journal.
+ Finally, arrange these qualities according to their importance to those outside your family circle. Write this series in your journal.

Reflect on the similarities and differences of these lists and write your thoughts in the journal. Close with a prayer of petition, and blow out the candle.

✧ Engage in an imaginary dialog with Frédéric. (If you choose, you may want to write this.) At the beginning, close your eyes and invite the young Frédéric to enter into conversation with you. Speak to him about

✦ his parents, their personal qualities and their experiences of revolution, war, and political turmoil
✦ his brothers and sisters, those who lived and those who died
✦ the relocation of his family from one place to another

Share with Frédéric the familial experiences of your own life when young: political unrest, wars, domestic happiness or sorrow, uprootings, charitable excursions on which you accompanied your parents. Ask Frédéric to be your companion as you read about his life. Compose a prayer to him to use regularly in beginning a meditation exercise.

✧ Reread the "Frédéric's Words" section. Underline the word or phrase that means the most to you. Reflect on the following questions:

✦ What "borderline situation" was I born into?
✦ Would my character suffer from too much wealth? Too much poverty?
✦ Whom can I relate to and serve most easily because of my life situation?

Within the next two days, find a friend with whom you can share your reflections.

✧ Read the "God's Word" section that follows. Write down three things that you have learned from your father and three things that you have learned from your mother. Write down three ways in which you honor your father and three ways in which you honor your mother. Do something for them this week that shows your gratitude and respect for them.

God's Word

My child, keep your father's commandment,
and do not forsake your mother's teaching.

Bind them upon your heart always;
tie them around your neck.
When you walk, they will lead you;
when you lie down, they will watch over you;
and when you awake, they will talk with you.

(Proverbs 6:20–22)

Closing prayer: Loving God, thank you for my parents. Thank you for all they have given me from the instant of my conception to this moment in time. Thank you for the gift of your compassion and love. Bless my parents, now and forever, with happiness, joy, and peace.

✧ Meditation 2 ✧

Finding Examples, Mentors, and Patrons

Theme: In the journey of life we need helpers—people who guide, encourage, and challenge us; people who model for us the kind of sojourners we desire to be.

Opening prayer: Jesus, holy friend, let me imitate you so that others may imitate me.

About Frédéric

Frédéric acknowledged the need for, and influence of, many people, living and deceased, as examples, mentors, and patrons in his life. Looking back on his life as a student, he wrote:

> For, young as I was then, with consciousness of my weakness and uncertainty of my future, I especially looked for support, advice and example among that society of intelligent and hardworking Christians, most happy to discover among the oldest of them that they did not disdain to accept me as a brother. (Dirvin, trans. and ed., *Letters*, p. 182)

Frédéric attributed his faith, determination, perseverance, and courage to the example of his parents. He attested also to

36

the daily religious example of two whom he called his "second fathers": André-Marie Ampère and Emmanuel Bailly.

In 1831, as a young student in Paris, Frédéric went to visit the home of the noted physicist Ampère. The elder Ampère invited Ozanam to reside in his home as a boarder while Ampère's own son was traveling in Germany. Frédéric enjoyed the meals, the amiable conversations, and the more serious work that took place in this household. But one day, weary from his own studies, Frédéric was out for a walk and stopped by the parish church of Saint Etienne du Mont. There he saw Ampère kneeling, saying his rosary, rapt in attention. The effect of this scene was profound. Frédéric later wrote, "'The rosary of Ampère . . . did more for me than all the books and sermons put together'" (Des Rivières, *Ozanam*, p. 34).

Emmanuel Bailly, also an older gentleman, was the proprietor of a printing press and the publisher of the *Catholic Tribune*, a newspaper published three times a week and distributed gratis to anyone who would read it. He opened his spacious office as a meeting space to the group of students that Ozanam had assembled around himself.

> [Bailly] was a poor man, but whenever there was a service to be rendered to the cause of truth, or to the young, he contrived somehow to find the necessary means. (O'Meara, *Life and Works*, p. 55)

It was under Bailly's auspices that the group moved from lively discussion of the issues of the day to the decision to actively serve the poor.

When that decision had been made, Frédéric sought out Sr. Rosalie Rendu, a Daughter of Charity of Saint Vincent de Paul who worked with the poor in the Mouffetard district of Paris. She became the mentor for his apostolic work as a layman. She taught him how to minister to the poor with love, respecting their dignity as human beings created in God's image and likeness. She instructed him that, above all, he was not to judge the poor. It was Sister Rosalie who fostered Frédéric's knowledge of and devotion to Saint Vincent de Paul and who first exemplified for him Vincentian spirituality.

Another of Frédéric's outstanding mentors was his spiritual director, Fr. J. B. Marduel, a priest of deep sanctity who was apparently gifted with the ability to read people's souls. Marduel was able to penetrate the clouds of darkness and confusion to a clearer, truer reality. He was of great benefit to someone of Frédéric's sensitivity.

The year 1837 was difficult for Frédéric. He found himself greatly distressed, and he approached his spiritual director at that time, pouring out his misery and confusion.

> "What do you think he said to me? He answered me in the words of the apostle: *Gaudete in Domino semper* (Rejoice in the Lord always). You will admit that it was a strange reply. A poor fellow has just had the greatest misfortune which can befall him in the spiritual order, that of offending God; the greatest misfortune which could befall him in the natural order, that of losing his father; he has an aged and infirm mother, whose every movement, every look, every expression he watches from day to day to see how long she is likely to be spared to him; . . . he is, over and above all this, a prey to anxiety about a most precarious future, overpowered with troubles and business of a most disagreeable nature; if he falls back upon himself in order to escape from what is painful without, he finds nothing but imperfections, weakness, and faults . . . and in the teeth of all this he is told, not to be resigned, to take comfort, but to rejoice—*gaudete semper!*" (O'Meara, *Life and Works*, pp. 103–104)

Frédéric delighted in the boldness of his director's response to him.

Pause: Who are your current examples, mentors, and patrons?

Frédéric's Words

Frédéric wrote this about his patron, Saint Vincent de Paul:

> A patron . . . is a model one must strive to imitate, as he himself imitated the model of Jesus Christ. He is a life to

be carried on, a heart in which one's own heart is enkindled, an intelligence from which light should be sought; he is a model on earth and a protector in heaven. A twofold devotion is owed him, imitation and invocation. . . .

Saint Vincent de Paul . . . has an immense advantage by reason of the nearness of the time when he lived, the infinite variety of benefits he bestowed, and the universality of admiration he inspires. The great souls who come nearest to God assume something of the prophetic. Without a doubt Saint Vincent de Paul had an anticipated vision of the evils and needs of our age: he was not a man to build on sand, nor to build for two days.

The benediction of the fourth commandment is upon the head of the saints; they honored their heavenly Father here below, and they will have long life. An earthly immortality is accorded them in their works. . . . The star of Saint Vincent de Paul, risen much later on the horizon, is not destined, surely, to accomplish a shorter career. Let us work in his light: let us honor our Father in this *patron* so worthy of love, and we shall live long. We shall perhaps see one day the children of our old age find ample shade under this institution whose frail beginnings we have seen. (Dirvin, trans. and ed., *Letters*, p. 143)

Reflection

Contemporary professionals tell us that we all have models—people we have imitated or in whose image we strive to pattern our life. We have, consciously or unconsciously, picked up their mannerisms and phrases, imbibed their attitudes and values.

Frédéric sought out models and mentors among "intelligent and hardworking Christians." He knew that was what his age called for and what he personally needed. He found models and mentors among the clergy, the religious, and the laypersons of his time.

Frédéric remained open to the providential, and sometimes unexpected, solutions to his problems, as was shown in his residence with M. Ampère, the patronage of M. Bailly, the mentoring of Sister Rosalie, and the encouragement of his spiritual director. Frédéric Ozanam invites us to reflect on those persons who have been examples, mentors, and patrons for us, whose qualities we hope to pass on in return.

✧ What do you think of the following statements?
✦ Heroism necessitates selflessness.
✦ Mentorship necessitates solid, sound guidance.
✦ Patronage necessitates persistent influence.
Take one of these—heroism, mentorship, or patronage—and write six additional elements that characterize this activity. Why is the one you selected important to you right now?

✧ Imitation is one of the primary ways Christians learn, live, and pass on the Gospel. Reflect on those persons that you have imitated as you reflect on the following verses of Scripture:
✦ "Be imitators of me, as I am of Christ" (1 Corinthians 11:1).
✦ "I appeal to you, then, be imitators of me" (1 Corinthians 4:16).
✦ "Brothers and sisters, join in imitating me, and observe those who live according to the example you have in us" (Philippians 3:17).
✦ "For you yourselves know how you ought to imitate us" (2 Thessalonians 3:7).
✦ "Be examples to the flock" (1 Peter 5:3).
Write your own litany honoring those who have modeled the faith for you, for example: For the compassion of John, I thank you God. For the wisdom of Mary, I thank you God. For the serenity of Charles, I thank you God. For the zeal of Ann, I thank you God.

✧ Perhaps there is something distressing or particularly overwhelming in your life right now that you are being invited to disclose to another wise and mature person in order to receive some guidance. Make the appropriate inquiries and arrangements to do this. Spend a limited amount of time writing down the things you want to say; do not overextend this time! Spend a quiet hour in prayer with this person, sitting or walking, inviting the spirit into this situation. When you return from this time of sharing, arrange some things on a table or shelf that represent the new grace given.

✧ Take some time to pray for those persons who are closest to you. Write down their names, or gather their pictures around you. Ask yourself these questions:

✦ How am I an example of (name an important quality) to this person?
✦ What does this person really need from me, as a mentor, at this time?
✦ What things am I pleased about in our relationship?
✦ What dimensions need improvement?

As you finish your prayer, recall each person and say a special prayer for them.

God's Word

[Jesus said, "The Reign of God] is like a mustard seed, which, when sown upon the ground, is the smallest of all the seeds on earth; yet when it is sown it grows up and becomes the greatest of all shrubs, and puts forth large branches, so that the birds of the air can make nests in its shade." (Mark 4:31–32)

Closing prayer: We pray as Frédéric prayed, "May our whole life be spent under the patronage of those to whom we consecrated our youth: Vincent de Paul, the Virgin Mary, and Jesus Christ our Savior" (Dirvin, trans. and ed., *Letters*, p. 114).

✧ Meditation 3 ✧

Passion for Truth

Theme: We are called to be people of truth—to live, sustain, and proclaim it.

Opening prayer: Jesus, you are the way, the truth, and the life. May I come to know your truth and put it into action with faith and love.

About Frédéric

A man appeared before Saint Peter, who asked him, "Where are your wounds?" The man replied, "I have no wounds." To which Peter rejoined, "Was there no passion in your life, no cause in which you spent and risked yourself that would invite scars?"

Frédéric had a passion in his life—the passion for truth. He had the scars to prove it—scars sustained because of the promise he had made to God to give his life to the service of the truth. Frédéric's passion for truth manifested itself in his loving adherence to the Catholic faith; in his professional work of study, writing, and teaching; and in his ministry with other Vincentians to the needs of poor people.

Three incidences from Frédéric's relationship with the students of the Sorbonne illustrate his integrity in relation to the truth. On one occasion, a student rewrote the posted announcements of Frédéric's course of foreign literature to read "Course of Theology." Frédéric was informed of the prank before entering the lecture hall. He said nothing until just before the end of class.

> "Gentlemen, I have not the *honour* to be a theologian, but I have the happiness to be a Christian; the happiness to believe and the ambition to devote my mind, my heart, and all my strength to the service of truth." (Baunard, *Correspondence,* p. 226)

His remarks received a loud, sustained applause. Frédéric's passion for the truth showed itself not only in his clarity of thought, but also in the approach he took as a Christian to the course material in literature.

At another time, one of his students had to withdraw from his course. Frédéric found the following note at his office:

> "Sir, . . . it is impossible not to believe what is so convincingly expressed. If it can give you some satisfaction, may I even say, happiness, learn then that before listening to you I did not believe. What many sermons have failed to do you have done in one lecture, you have made me a Christian. Accept, sir, the expression of my joy and gratitude." (Baunard, *Correspondence,* p. 201)

Frédéric's passion for truth came across in his conviction and eloquence.

Frédéric never allowed attacks on the church or religion to go unchallenged, especially those that reflected the position that the church and its teachings impeded human progress. One day he was on a board of examiners for a student's degree. The student had regaled the others with his eloquence and Italian charm. When it came Frédéric's turn to examine the student, Frédéric said:

> "Sir, . . . I admire your ability but not your knowledge. You have not done justice to the Fathers of the Church in accusing them of having arrested the course of civilisation. You are not right in that; you would have done better on the contrary in asserting that they quickened its march." (Baunard, *Correspondence,* p. 208)

Frédéric's colleagues immediately saw the truth of his assertion and agreed with him. They recognized, however, that Frédéric alone had challenged the assumptions of the student's thesis.

Years later, as he looked back over his life, Frédéric wrote,

"If anything . . . can console me for leaving this world with my work unfinished, it is that I have never worked to win the approbation of men, but solely in the service of truth." (Baunard, *Correspondence*, p. 402)

Pause: Do you have a passion for truth? Do you have any scars to prove it?

Frédéric's Words

Frédéric wrote the following to Amélie, his wife:

Now then, my well-beloved, in comparing and discussing all the diverse reflections, I am strong in this belief in my vocation of which all the events of my latest years render me more certain. Truth has no need of me, but I have need of it. The cause of Christian knowledge, the cause of the faith, is what I hold to the roots of my heart; and in any way I can serve it, I will be worthily employed the years accounted me on the earth. Since it is threatened, and since literature is the field of battle where the quarrel is drawn, and teaching is a large part of it, and Paris is the French city and perhaps for the world where the debates of ideas seem to be decided, and Providence by the advice of my friends and family and the irresistible inspiration I experience has put me on the rampart, I shall not come down from it. Good can be done here which would be impossible elsewhere. I will make use of that power of the public word with which they have wished to honor me, and I will grow firmer in making it certain and prolonging its effectiveness by marshaling and leading young Christian youth into the path of worthwhile study. I will write also so as not lose in fleeting speech the little given me to expound to men. (Dirvin, trans. and ed., *Letters*, p. 357)

Reflection

Frédéric's passion and mission was for truth and the service of truth. His world had been one fraught with social unrest and revolutionary transitions. It was paradoxically a time of apathy and indifference and of strong positions and political fervor. In this milieu Frédéric was willing to question interpretations and promote discussion. He countered duplicity and hypocrisy wherever he saw it. He believed the truths of his faith were absolutes, made clearer through prayer and study.

Frédéric, no doubt, would find great difficulty in today's society that shuns absolutes, espouses only opinions with varying credibility, and holds that truth is relative. Frédéric would be among the first to confront such a perspective. He would see it for its defective reasoning and dire consequences.

There is a moral virtue called veracity that falls under the cardinal virtue of justice. Veracity, or truth, is "the virtue which consists in showing oneself true in deeds and truthful in words, and in guarding against duplicity, dissimulation, and hypocrisy." (*Catechism of the Catholic Church*, no. 2468, p. 652). Frédéric invites us to this veracity, this integrity, this passion for the truth.

✧ Reflect on these words of Saint Bernard of Clairvaux:

There are many who seek knowledge for the sake of knowledge: that is curiosity.

There are others who desire to know in order that they may themselves be known: that is vanity.

But there are some who seek knowledge in order to serve and edify others: and that is love.

✧ Frédéric wrote, "Truth has no need of me; but I have need of it." Can you say this of yourself? Where do you stand on duplicity, fabrication, hypocrisy? Take some time for meditation on the situations of deceit that are part of your world. Where is the battlefield in which you are called to witness to the truth?

✧ Plan to do a meditation for a week on the following two questions:

✦ What transcendent values, or truths, do you see people living by today?
✦ What transcendent values, or truths, are notable by their absence?

Take your journal and visit a mall, a church, a park, a social center (school, day care, or senior center), an office, or a hospital. Take at least fifteen minutes to contemplate what is happening in these places and its impact on you. Then respond to the following questions at the end of the week, evaluating your experience:

✦ What was confirmed for you?
✦ What new insights did you gain?
✦ What changes should you make in your own values, attitudes, and actions?

✧ Frédéric wrote, "Let us not confine our beliefs to a realm of speculation and theory, let us take them seriously, and then our life will be their continued expression" (Dirvin, trans. and ed., *Letters*, p. 26). Are there some truths you hold that remain in the realm of theory? Are they the kind that need to be translated into practice? Do you have a passion for veracity? Do you see how it falls under the cardinal virtue of justice? Write a prayer for your own use, petitioning for a greater ability to live the truth.

God's Word

Who is wise and understanding among you? Show by your good life that your works are done with gentleness born of wisdom. But if you have bitter envy and selfish ambition in your hearts, do not be boastful and false to the truth. Such wisdom does not come down from above, but is earthly, unspiritual, devilish. For where there is envy and selfish ambition, there will also be disorder and wickedness of every kind. But the wisdom from above is first pure, then peaceable, gentle, willing to yield, full of mercy and good fruits, without a trace of partiality or hypocrisy. (James 3:13–17)

Closing prayer: God of truth, God of light, grant me the grace to be true to you, true to myself, and true to others in word and action, after the example of Frédéric Ozanam.

✧ Meditation 4 ✧

The Sacred Fire of Faith

Theme: Faith is like a sacred fire, burning within and enkindling the works of charity. It is God's self-revelation and our free response to it.

Opening prayer: "'I believe; help my unbelief!'" (Mark 9:24)

About Frédéric

A friend wrote about Frédéric:

> "He has the sacred fire. There is such an air of interior conviction in this man, that without the appearance of doing so, he convinces and moves you." (Baunard, *Correspondence*, p. 201)

Frédéric's sacred fire was faith. Faith for Frédéric Ozanam was indeed a living reality that permeated his entire being; it was his "second sight." Yet, it was a hard-won gift.

When Frédéric was sixteen years old, he suffered a crisis of faith. He described it at length:

> But I must go into some detail about a painful period of my life, a period which began when I was in rhetoric and ended this past year. From hearing about unbelievers and unbelief, I asked myself why I believed. I doubted, dear

friend, and although I wanted to believe and resisted the doubt, I read every book where religion was proven and not one of them satisfied me completely. I would believe for a month or two on the authority of certain reasoning: an objection would leap to my mind, and I would doubt again. Oh! How I suffered, for I wanted to be religious. I buried myself in Valla. Valla did not satisfy me. My faith was not firm, and meanwhile I preferred to believe without reason than to doubt, because it tormented me too much.

I began philosophy. The thesis of certitude upset me completely. I believed for an instant I could doubt my existence and could not. I finally decided to believe. Little by little everything reasserted itself, and today I believe on the authority of the idea of cause. (Dirvin, trans. and ed., *Letters*, p. 11)

How was this crisis of faith resolved? Frédéric literally was brought to his knees. Thanks to a friend, we know that

"In the darkest hour of trial, which had become for him actual physical pain, the young student appealed to the mercy of God for light and peace. He threw himself on his knees before the Most Blessed Sacrament, and there in tears and in all humility, he promised Our Lord that, if He would deign to make the lamp of truth shine in his sight, he would consecrate his life to its defence." (Baunard, *Correspondence*, pp. 10–11)

Like a fog suddenly lifted by a strong wind, Frédéric rose from his knees consoled and at peace. Frédéric's mind was free from doubt; his eyes of faith were cleared of their scales. Like Saint Paul on the road to Damascus, Frédéric sought out his Ananias on a street called Straight in the person of Fr. Joseph Noirot, professor of philosophy at the College of Lyon and a family friend. As Ananias taught Paul, Noirot taught Frédéric.

"Then it was that the teaching of a priest, who was also a philosopher, came to my rescue. He dispelled the clouds and illumined the darkness of my thoughts. From then I believed with faith grounded on the rock. Touched by such a grace I promised God to consecrate my days to the service of truth. That restored peace to my soul." (Baunard, *Correspondence*, pp. 9–10)

As time went on, Frédéric proclaimed his faith openly and staunchly during a time of great complexity in French history. He proclaimed the faith in the lecture halls of universities, in newspaper and journal articles, in the homes of the poor, among friends, with acquaintances, and in discussions with foes. For Frédéric, faith was truth lived out.

Pause: Is faith a sacred fire for you?

Frédéric's Words

"Ah! my dear friend, what a troublous, but what an instructive time it is, through which we are passing! We may perish, but we must not regret having lived in it. Let us learn from it. Let us learn, first of all, to defend our belief without hating our adversaries, to appreciate those who do not think as we do, to recognize that there are Christians in every camp, and that God can be served now as always! Let us complain less of our times and more of ourselves. Let us not be discouraged, let us be better." (Baunard, *Correspondence*, p. 304)

Reflection

Frédéric knew faith to be the beginning and the foundation of his spiritual life; yet he had to grasp this anew at different stages of his maturation. Although he had first been taught at the knees of his parents, Frédéric needed to grapple with the truth of the faith as he developed intellectually and morally. Indeed, coupled with the typical quests of adolescence were the added challenges of an atheistic, scientific, and rationalistic mindset common to his era.

Yet the grace of the theological virtues of faith, hope, and charity were ever at work in him and became the enduring core of his life.

✧ Frédéric attributes the foundation of his faith to his parents.

"In the midst of an age of scepticism, God gave me the grace to be born in the true faith. As a child I listened at the feet of a Christian father and a saintly mother." (Baunard, *Correspondence*, p. 9)

To whom do you attribute your faith? Are you able to voice sentiments of gratitude? Recite Psalm 100.

✧ Read over the "God's Word" section. Are you being called to be like Ananias for Paul or Noirot for Frédéric, for a person younger in the faith who is struggling with belief in God? Think about teaching religious education, working in an RCIA program, or becoming a confirmation sponsor in your parish.

✧ Examine your life and the nature of any dichotomies you experience. In what areas are you not living by faith? Do you tend to insulate your faith from the rest of your life? What must you do to integrate your faith and your life? Do you grapple with a tenet of the faith? How does this affect you?

✧ Open yourself in prayer to the Holy Spirit so that the gift of faith may grow in you. The gifts of understanding and knowledge perfect faith; pray for the illumination of these gifts.

✧ Reread the "Frédéric's Words" section. Underline the phrases that are most significant to you. Take the initiative this week to share Frédéric's words with three people, or to have these words published in a local paper or publication.

God's Word

Now there was a disciple in Damascus named Ananias. The Lord said to him in a vision, "Ananias." He answered, "Here I am, Lord." The Lord said to him, "Get up and go to the street called Straight, and at the house of Judas look for a man of Tarsus named Saul. At this moment he is praying, and he has seen in a vision a man named Ananias come in and lay his hands on him so that he might regain his sight." . . . So Ananias went and entered the house. He laid his hands on Saul and said, "Brother Saul, the Lord Jesus, who appeared to you on your way here, has sent me so that you may regain your sight and be filled with the Holy Spirit." And immediately something like scales fell from his eyes, and his sight was restored. Then he got up and was baptized, and after taking some food, he regained his strength. (Acts 9:10–19)

Closing prayer: Saving God, you have said that you have come to cast fire on the earth. Cast the fire of faith into my heart, that it may burn there and enkindle the works of charity.

✦ **Meditation 5** ✦

Cultivating Humility

Theme: Humility is walking in truth.

Opening prayer: Jesus, you who have walked among us healing and teaching, remove from me everything and anything that bespeaks of pride and arrogance.

About Frédéric

Frédéric was a man who treasured the virtue of humility. The principal reason for Frédéric's fondness for and cultivation of humility was his passion for truth. The following quote from Saint Teresa of Ávila represents the mind and conduct of Frédéric:

> Once I was pondering why our Lord was so fond of this virtue of humility, and this thought came to me—in my opinion not as a result of reflection but suddenly: It is because God is supreme Truth; and to be humble is to walk in truth, for it is a very deep truth that of ourselves we have nothing good but only misery and nothingness. Whoever does not understand this walks in falsehood. The more anyone understands it the more he pleases the supreme Truth because he is walking in truth. (Kieran Kavanaugh and Otilio Rodriguez, trans., *Teresa of Ávila: The Interior Castle*, p. 165)

In his adult life, Frédéric was able to discern quickly where he was called to use his gifts and where he was not. In 1848, a friend, Théophile Foisset, and some others hoped that Frédéric would get involved in national politics. They wanted him to run for a seat in the parliament. Their expectation was that Frédéric Ozanam would emerge as one of the bright and energetic leaders of the new political order. Frédéric replied that he knew his energies were best spent at the university and not in the chambers of politics.

Throughout his life Frédéric tended to judge himself rather severely, but he treated others quite differently. This was especially true in regard to the poor and the powerless for whom he showed the greatest tenderness and respect. He always removed his top hat upon entering their homes and said cordially, "I am here to serve you." Frédéric never judged them or their condition. He used his judgment, rather, to promote their welfare. He would do whatever he could for their immediate good, and then, celebrated professor and esteemed author though he was, Frédéric would sit down and spend time chatting with these poor and uneducated persons about their own concerns and interests.

What Frédéric discovered from these visits to the homes of the poor was that he, the evangelizer, became evangelized. He expressed this very well in a talk he delivered to the Society of Saint Vincent de Paul of Florence, Italy.

> "How often has it not happened that being weighed down by some interior trouble, uneasy as to my poor state of health, I entered the home of the poor confided to my care; there, face to face with so many miserable poor, who had so much more to complain of, I felt reproached for my depression, I felt better able to bear sorrow, and I gave thanks to that unhappy one, the contemplation of whose sufferings had consoled and fortified me! How could I avoid henceforward loving him the more!" (Baunard, *Correspondence*, pp. 343–344)

Frédéric's humility, which engaged him with the poor, also brought him greater strength and love—indeed, greater humility.

Frédéric saw humility as mandatory for organizations as well as for individuals. He emphasized this virtue and characteristic in regard to the Society of Saint Vincent de Paul. Like his patron, Saint Vincent de Paul, who called his community the "Little Company," Frédéric called his association of charity the "Little Society of Saint Vincent de Paul." Concerning humility, he wrote:

> "It would be well to lay down this principle: that humility is as obligatory on associations as on individuals; and to support it by the example of Saint Vincent de Paul. . . . Our guiding rule should be neither to force ourselves on the public gaze, nor to conceal ourselves from those who may wish to find us.
>
> "It was prophesied for us that publicity meant death; it is to our obscurity that we owe our life, our development, and whatever good work we have done; thanks to it we have been able to falsify the prophets of evil." (Baunard, *Correspondence*, p. 130)

Obscurity coupled with good works became a mode of corporate humility, a way of walking in the truth.

Pause: Are you hard on yourself and easy on others? How does each accord with the truth?

Frédéric's Words

Frédéric responded to his friend, Théophile Foisset:

> "You are quite wrong, my dear friend, in thinking that I am one of the men of the moment. I have never been so keenly conscious of my weakness and my ineffectiveness. I am less qualified than almost any other, to deal with those questions which are agitating men's minds! I mean questions of labour, wages, commerce, administration, which are more important than any political controversy. . . . I am not a man of action, nor am I suited for Parliament or for the platform. If I can do anything however small, it is in my University chair or perhaps in the seclu-

sion of my library, in extracting from Philosophy and from History thoughts which I can put before young men, before troubled and vacillating minds, in order to steady, to encourage, to rally them together, in the confusion of the present and the terrible uncertainty of the future." (Baunard, *Correspondence*, pp. 258–259)

Reflection

Frédéric judged himself rather harshly. His writings provide many self-descriptions which convey such incriminations. Although many considered Frédéric great, he considered himself little. Although many thought him to be extraordinarily good, he thought himself to be a poor sinner in the sight of God. Frédéric believed that his talents were due to his "industry" in collaboration with God's grace. In his mind he saw himself to be a weak and feeble human being.

From Frédéric's personal experience with the poor, he understood that humility is an essential virtue for ministers to the poor because it clothes them with the same garment worn by Jesus, the evangelizer of the poor. Humility emboldened Frédéric to minister to the poor with gentleness and cordiality. Humility put the poor at ease. And this humility allowed Frédéric to accept whatever came his way in return.

✧ Reflect on the Gospel passages in which Jesus enters the homes of others. Note that he usually shares a meal, teaches, or heals. Read and ponder your favorite story. Ask yourself: How is the humility of Jesus shown here? What can I learn from his manner and action?

✧ How do you see humility for yourself in today's society? Would you say that you are a humble person? Would you say that you walk in the truth?

✧ Frédéric knew that some positions did not match the talents he had been given. Reread the "Frédéric's Words" section. Reflect on your own situation.

✦ Have you ever been encouraged to take a position that did not fit your talents? How did you respond? Was it difficult?

✦ Have you ever been encouraged to take a position that did match your talents? How did you respond? How did you show your gratitude?

✦ Have you already found yourself in a position that did not match your talents? What did you do about it?

At the end of this reflection time, pray Psalm 86.

✧ What do you think of humility as an obligation for an association? Can a charitable organization realistically cultivate such a virtue in today's milieu? Do you know one that has attempted it? Did it meet with success? Did it meet with failure? Does today's culture militate against humility? Does today's culture provide an environment for humility? Share your thoughts on this with someone else today.

God's Word

When he noticed how the guests chose the places of honor, he told them a parable. "When you are invited by someone to a wedding banquet, do not sit down at the place of honor, in case someone more distinguished than you has been invited by your host; and the host who invited both of you may come and say to you, 'Give this person your place,' and then in disgrace you would start to take the lowest place. But when you are invited, go and sit down at the lowest place, so that when your host comes, he may say to you, 'Friend, move up higher'; then you will be honored in the presence of all who sit at the table with you. For all who exalt themselves will be humbled, and those who humble themselves will be exalted."

He said also to the one who had invited him, "When you give a luncheon or a dinner, do not invite your friends or your brothers or your relatives or rich neighbors, in case they may invite you in return, and you would be repaid. But when you give a banquet, invite the poor, the crippled, the lame, and the blind. And you will be blessed, because they cannot repay you, for you will be repaid at the resurrection of the righteous." (Luke 14:7–14)

Closing prayer: Jesus, meek and humble of heart, grant me the grace to be like you. Grant me the grace to be humble in thought, word, and deed.

Marriage

Theme: "The grace of the sacrament [of marriage] thus perfects the human love of the spouses, strengthens their indissoluble unity, and sanctifies them on the way to eternal life" (*Catechism of the Catholic Church*, no. 1661, p. 463).

Opening prayer: O Loving God, strengthen all married couples in their love for each other. Sanctify them in their journey to you.

About Frédéric

In 1978, Pope John Paul I told an amusing but inspiring story about Frédéric Ozanam at one of his general audiences.

> "Last century there was in France a great professor, Frédéric Ozanam. He taught at the Sorbonne, and was so eloquent, so capable! His friend was Lacordaire, who said: 'He is so gifted, he is so good, he will become a priest, he will become a great bishop, this fellow!' No! He met a nice girl and they got married. Lacordaire was disappointed and said: 'Poor Ozanam! He too has fallen into the trap!' But two years later, Lacordaire came to Rome, and was received by Pius IX. 'Come, come, Father,' he said, 'I have always heard that Jesus established seven sacraments. Now you come along and change everything.

You tell me that He established six sacraments, and a trap! No, Father, marriage is not a trap—it is a great sacrament!'" (*The Message of John Paul I*, p. 110)

It was love at first sight for Frédéric. He met the woman of his dreams, Amélie Soulacroix, in the home of her parents. Amélie's father was the rector of the Academy of Lyon. Frédéric's dear friend and mentor, Fr. Joseph Noirot, had set up the meeting of Frédéric and Amélie without either of them knowing it; the priest was matchmaker!

Frédéric wrote to his good friend, François Lallier:

"You must find me completely infatuated, head over heels in love, but I cannot hide it, although I sometimes laugh at myself. I really thought my heart was immune." (Des Rivières, *Ozanam*, p. 89)

It was quite obvious that Frédéric was smitten—his heart was far from immune!

Frédéric and Amélie exchanged gold lockets during their engagement. Each locket contained a lock of the other's hair. They wore these as long as they lived.

After a formal engagement of some six months, Frédéric and Amélie were married in Lyon. Frédéric described the wedding and his feelings in a letter to François Lallier.

Last Wednesday, June 23, at ten o'clock in the morning, in the church of Saint Nizier, your friend knelt; at the altar was his older brother, raising his priestly hands, and at his feet, his young brother, making the responses to the liturgical prayers. Beside him you would have seen a young girl, in white and wearing a veil, pious as an angel, and already—she lets me say it—attendant and affectionate as a friend. Happier even than I, her family surrounding her, and yet at the same time she welcomed all the family heaven has left me here below; and my old comrades, my brothers of Saint Vincent de Paul, numerous acquaintances, filling the choir and peopling the nave. It was beautiful, and strangers who chanced upon it were seen to be profoundly moved. I could scarcely restrain great but delightful tears, while I felt the divine blessing descend upon me with the sacred words. (Dirvin, trans. and ed., *Letters*, p. 269)

Two years after his marriage, Frédéric wrote to Amélie:

Come, then, my well-beloved, my dove, my angel, come
into my arms, against my heart, come bringing me yours
so pure and generous: come and God bless you that after
two years we love each other a thousand times more than
on the first day! (Dirvin, trans. and ed., *Letters*, p. 358)

On 23 June 1853, the twelfth anniversary of their marriage, Frédéric composed a poem in honor of his wife, Amélie.
He wrote it in the small town of San Jacopo, near Pisa, Italy; it
was the last summer of his life.

Stranded on a distant rock our little barque awaits the
saving tide to bring it into port. The Madonna, to whom
the vessel is dedicated, seems deaf to our appeals and the
Infant Jesus slumbers!

It is twelve years to-day since we set out on our voyage full of hope; garlands decorated thy head. To bless the
voyage, a little fair-haired angel soon appeared at the
stern.

Since then the heavens have grown dark and the
storms have blown our little skiff hither and thither by
night and day. But neither the trials of the tempest nor the
hardships of the climate could extinguish our love.

Dearest companion of the exile whom God allotted to
me, I have no further fear in your sweet care. Already the
merciful eyes of the Virgin Mother are turning to us: the
Infant Jesus will soon awaken.

Drawn by His hand into a calm sea we shall reach at
length the shore where our longing, loving friends are
waiting to receive us.

(Baunard, *Correspondence*, p. 392)

Throughout the years of his marriage, on the twenty-third
of each month, Frédéric never failed to give Amélie flowers
for their anniversary. Even on his death bed, Frédéric made
certain that Amélie received her bouquet. Flowers were but a
small sign of the deep affection and love that burned in his
heart for Amélie.

After Frédéric was entombed in the Church of Saint-
Joseph-des-Carmes, at the Institut Catholique, people often

saw Amélie and Marie, their daughter, slipping down to the crypt with fresh flowers. Frédéric was on her mind and in her heart until the day she died.

Pause: How do you express love to those who are most dear to you?

Frédéric's Words

Six years before he himself was wed, Frédéric wrote to a dear friend, a confrere in the Society of Saint Vincent de Paul, about the man's coming marriage.

> The great action you are contemplating at present will only serve to redouble your zeal and your strength. "When two or three are gathered together in my name," says the Savior, "there am I in the midst of them." It is in that divine name that you will prepare to unite yourself to a wise and pious wife: the promise will be accomplished in you both. In giving your love to someone who will be justifiably dear, you will not withdraw it from the poor and miserable whom you loved first. Love possesses something of the divine nature, which gives itself without diminishing, which shares itself without division, which multiplies itself, which is present in many places at once, and whose intensity is increased in the measure that it gains in extension. In your wife you will first love God, whose admirable and precious work she is, and then humanity, that race of Adam whose pure and lovable daughter she is. You will draw comfort from her tenderness on bad days, you will find courage in her example in perilous times, you will be her guardian angel, she will be yours. You will then no longer experience the weaknesses, discouragements and terrors which have seized upon you at certain times of your life: for you will no longer be alone. You will never be alone again, your virtue will be shared in legitimate hope, the alliance you are about to contract will be an immortal alliance: what God joins together, what He has insisted no man separate, He will not

Himself separate, and in heaven He will invest with the same glory those who here below were companions in the same exile. (Dirvin, trans. and ed., *Letters*, p. 72)

Reflection

Frédéric had given serious thought to being a priest. His friend, Père Henri Lacordaire wanted Frédéric to join him. Frédéric said, "I would have time to see . . . whether divine Providence might not wish to open the doors of the Order of Saint Dominic to me" (Dirvin, trans. and ed., *Letters*, p. 178).

Frédéric expended much energy in prayer, reflection, and consultation in discerning God's will. Fr. Joseph Noirot, the priest who knew Frédéric the longest, and better than anyone else did, finally said to him, "'Get married, my dear young man, get married'" (O'Meara, *Life and Works*, p. 133). Frédéric resolved the internal struggle. He experienced peace with the decision. It was God's will for him to remain a layman. He chose marriage as his vocation.

Frédéric gave himself unreservedly in the commitment to his wife. In spite of his multiple occupations and responsibilities, Amélie always held first priority in his life. He loved her dearly and truly shared his life with her. When God blessed them with their daughter, Marie, he spent countless hours with this baby who became the apple of his eye. Like many working parents, he sometimes regretted not being able to give her more time and attention.

✧ Reflect on your own path of discernment concerning your vocation, your primary commitment in life.
+ Did you have struggles?
+ Did you go through stages?
+ Did anyone help you along the way?
+ Were there events that became turning points?
+ Did you have the conviction that the choice was "of God"? How and when did this conviction come to you?
+ Do you have struggles in your present vocation?
+ Do you need to take action concerning these struggles? Do you need to be patient at this time?

✦ What do you hope for?
Reflect on the predominant quality, or grace, within your vocation. Compose a prayer to use as a morning offering this month that highlights this dominant quality or grace.

✧ Marriage takes on the cultural tone of the age. Reread Pope John Paul I's story: "Marriage is not a trap—it is a great sacrament." Why is marriage sometimes considered a trap? How is marriage a sacrament? Is the present culture an impediment to a healthy attitude toward marriage? What aspects of the present culture foster healthy marriages?

Call together a small group to answer these questions together. Before you go your separate ways, make a resolution, however small, to do something for the benefit of a married couple or for marriage in general this week.

✧ Frédéric gave his wife flowers every month on the anniversary of their marriage. Do you do something similar? Does your spouse do something similar? Reflect on the small but regular ways that you acknowledge your bond with each other and your appreciation.

✧ Pope John Paul II, in his apostolic letter of 1994 "Tertio Millennio Adveniente" says:

> There is a need to foster the recognition of the heroic virtues of men and women who have lived their Christian vocation in marriage. Precisely because we are convinced of the abundant fruits of holiness in the married state, we need to find the most appropriate means for discerning them and proposing them to the whole church as a model and encouragement for other Christian spouses. (*Origins*, 24 November 1994, p. 412)

Write a letter to the pope sharing with him instances in your marriage (or in the marriage of a couple you know well) that have demanded "heroic virtues." Tell him where and how you have experienced the "abundant fruits of holiness" as a couple, and the means that he can adopt that would enable him to discern them. Share with him any ideas you have for more effective communication in the church concerning the grace of marriage. Share this letter with a friend or an interested group. If the spirit so moves, contact your pastor or the bishop to see how you can respond to this papal call.

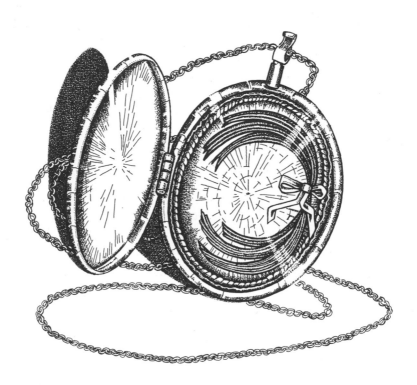

God's Word

"This is my commandment, that you love one another, as I have loved you. No one has greater love than this, to lay down one's life for one's friends. You are my friends if you do what I command you. I do not call you servants any longer, because the servant does not know what the master is doing; but I have called you friends, because I have made known to you everything that I have heard from [God]. You did not choose me but I chose you. And I appointed you to go and bear fruit, fruit that will last, so that [God] will give you whatever you ask . . . in my name. I am giving you these commandments so that you may love one another." (John 15:12–17)

Closing prayer: "[God of love, keep (name of couple)] always true to your commandments. Keep them faithful in marriage and let them be living examples of Christian life. Give them the strength which comes from the Gospel so that they may be witnesses of Christ to others" (*Rites of the Catholic Church,* vol. 1, no. 33, pp. 730–731).

Devotion to Mary

Theme: Devotion to Mary, the mother of God, was part of Frédéric Ozanam's life from childhood to death. He sought her intercession often.

Opening prayer: Hail Mary, full of grace, the Lord is with you.

About Frédéric

Nowhere in his writings does Frédéric Ozanam speak of a theology or a spirituality of Mary, the mother of God, but what does come forth loud and clear is his devotion to Mary.

Frédéric's devotion to Mary was directed particularly, but not exclusively, to Notre Dame de Fourviere, the patroness of his city of Lyon. The shrine to Our Lady sits on the hill of Fourviere overlooking the Saone river and the sprawling city of Lyon below. Devotion to Notre Dame de Fourviere can be traced back to the earliest years of Christianity. The shrine is built on the site of a temple of Venus. In later years when the death-dealing cholera was only miles from Lyon and hundreds were fleeing the city, others knelt at the shrine of Notre Dame de Fourviere and implored the mother of God to save their city. Their prayer was answered.

Frédéric's personal devotion to Mary was shown early in his life, and reappeared in various forms at different decades.

Frédéric began composing prose and poetry in Latin and French at thirteen years of age. At that time one of his favorite subjects was the praise of the Blessed Virgin Mary. When he was twenty-one years old and maturing, he still found Our Lady an appropriate intercessor. Kneeling at her altar, he prayed, and later wrote to a friend:

> "I have made a resolution of more complete moral reform during my remaining two years in the capital. I place my intentions under the auspices of our Divine Mother, trusting for the rest to my good will!" (Baunard, *Correspondence*, p. 98)

When he was thirty-two years old, his daughter was born. Frédéric considered her birth a response to the blessing and intercession of the mother of God. The little girl herself was given the name Marie.

In the last year of his life, while traveling with his family, Frédéric made a pilgrimage to Notre Dame de Buglosse, a shrine near the birthplace of his patron, Saint Vincent de Paul. Here Frédéric prayed for healing. He wrote of this pilgrimage:

> "The old sanctuary is made venerable by a statue of the Virgin Mary which attracts many pilgrims. We finished our pilgrimage there on Saturday morning, and had the consolation of receiving Holy Communion, asking God for the cure in which we all three are concerned. It is a very long while since I was so moved.
>
> ". . . I believed myself cured at that time, and it was rather for the purpose of thanks than for petition, that I made that pilgrimage. However, without wishing to attach any supernatural importance to anything that concerns me, I admit that one incident made a very deep impression on me. I went to Confession to a holy priest who does duty at the chapel of Notre Dame, and whose simplicity and great charity recalled at once our Saint Vincent de Paul. Now, that man of God, in the remarks which he made, spoke only of sufferings to be endured patiently, of resignation and submission to the will of God, however hard it might be! . . . Such language surprised me very much, as I was feeling well." (Baunard, *Correspondence*, p. 370)

Later that year, in Livorno, Italy, on the feast of the Assumption, Frédéric, three weeks away from death's door, insisted on walking to church. There he attended Mass and received Holy Communion. "'It may be my last walk in this world, and I desire that it shall be to pay a visit to my God and His Blessed Mother'" (Baunard, *Correspondence*, p. 400).

Frédéric died on the feast of the Birthday of the Blessed Virgin Mary, 8 September 1853. It seems fitting for this man to die on the feast of a woman to whom he had been greatly devoted all his life.

Pause: What place does devotion to Our Lady hold in your life? Has it changed as you have grown older?

Frédéric's Words

Frédéric wrote in 1845:

> "My friends have a great deal to do this year helping me to give thanks. After so many favors which fixed my vocation in this world and put an end to the scattering of my family, a new blessing has come to me, the greatest joy, probably, it is possible to experience here below! *I am a father!*
>
> "We prayed much; we begged for prayers on every side; never did we feel greater need of the Divine assistance! . . . Ah! what a moment that was when I heard the first cry of my child; when I beheld that little creature, but that immortal creature, which God has confided to me, who brought me so many delights and so many duties. . . . We have called her Marie, which is her mother's name, as well as that of the powerful protectress to whose intercession we attribute this happy birth. . . . We will begin her education early and, at the same time, she will begin ours; for I perceive that Heaven has sent her to us to teach us a great deal, and to make us better. I cannot look upon that sweet little face, so full of innocence and purity, without seeing there, less obliterated than in us, the sacred impress of the Creator. I cannot think of this imperishable soul, of which I shall have to

render an account, without feeling myself more penetrated with my duties. How could I dare teach her lessons that I did not practice? Could God have found a kinder way of instructing me, of correcting me, and setting my feet on the road to heaven?" (O'Meara, *Life and Works*, p. 186)

Reflection

Frédéric believed in the power of the mother of God. He often prayed to her for himself and for others. He believed in the power of Mary's intercession with her divine offspring. Devotion to her was woven into the various stages of Frédéric's life and was especially prominent in the poetic devotion of youth, the moral challenges of young adulthood, the transformation of becoming a parent, and the acceptance of suffering and impending death. Frédéric invites us to consider our own devotion to Mary and our trust in her intercession.

✧ Frédéric lived in a city which had a history of devotion to Mary. Center yourself in prayer and imagine your childhood. Was there a Marian ambiance in your environment? What statues, feast days, rituals, and hymns do you remember? Who brought to you a caring, maternal presence? Who would respond to your requests?

Say a special prayer of thanksgiving for these good influences in your young life. Sing a hymn you remember. Place a bouquet of flowers before a picture that recalls for you the influence of the mother of God.

✧ The name of Mary is a common one even today. On a piece of paper, write down all the Mary's you have known throughout your life, taking time to remember the relationship you had with them. As you finish your prayer, go through the list again, asking for a blessing on each one.

✧ Have you ever felt the power of Mary, the mother of God, in your life? Do you need to ask her intercession for a significant situation now? Compose a prayer for yourself to use in the next nine days. If possible, make a pilgrimage to a Marian shrine or to the statue of Mary in your parish church.

✧ Who are the blessed women in your life? Make a list of them. Choose one or several to whom you can make a special gesture of thanksgiving this week.

✧ Recite Mary's Magnificat. Pray it in thanksgiving for all the graces God has given you in your life.

God's Word

And Mary said,
"My soul magnifies the Lord,
    and my spirit rejoices in God my Savior,
for he has looked with favor on the lowliness
    of his servant.
Surely, from now on all generations will call me
    blessed;
for the Mighty One has done great things for me,
    and holy is his name.
His mercy is for those who fear him
    from generation to generation.
He has shown strength with his arm;
        he has scattered the proud in the thoughts of their
            hearts.
He has brought down the powerful from their thrones,
    and lifted up the lowly;
he has filled the hungry with good things,
    and sent the rich away empty.
He has helped his servant Israel,
    in remembrance of his mercy,
according to the promise he made to our ancestors,
    to Abraham and to his descendants forever."
                                    (Luke 1:46–55)

Closing prayer: Holy Mary, mother of God, pray for us
sinners now and at the hour of our death. Amen.

✧ Meditation 8 ✧

Divine Providence

Theme: "'We must respect the earth as the workshop of Providence'" (Baunard, *Correspondence*, p. 423).

Opening prayer: "'Our Father in heaven, / hallowed be your name. / Your kingdom come. / Your will be done, / on earth as it is in heaven'" (Matthew 6:9–10).

About Frédéric

Frédéric loved the out-of-doors. The earth spoke to him of the providence of God, and leisurely moments allowed him the time to appreciate the past, contemplate the present, and look with confidence toward the future.

Shortly after Marie was born, the family went to the country for a holiday. Frédéric wrote:

> "The quiet of the country affords me a leisure which I have not known for a long time. . . . The garden is large, the air is pure, the weather lovely. My wife is picking up her strength rapidly, and my child is opening out like a little flower. It is one of those moments of bliss which are not often granted to us in life, and which make us feel more keenly the goodness of Providence." (O'Meara, *Life and Works*, p. 187)

74

Two years before, he had written a letter to Amélie which again alludes to the workings of providence:

Three years ago, when the success of my teaching was uncertain, I did not falter. I did not listen to dictates of self-interest: I sought in my career knowledge only. I believe that it was God who thus inspired me, and made me act with a confidence that was foreign to my weak character. Then Providence led you into my path, and I offered you the sharing of a life poor, for long and perhaps ever obscure, but sanctified, ennobled by the cultivation of all that is beautiful: I offered you solitude far from all belonging to you, but with the tenderness of a heart which had never belonged to anyone but you. (Dirvin, trans. and ed., *Letters*, pp. 356–357)

Even before that, while still discerning his vocation, Frédéric had written:

"My future I leave in the hands of Providence. I shall accept willingly whatever place He will be pleased to assign me to, however lowly it may be. It will be always noble, if it be filled worthily." (Baunard, *Correspondence*, pp. 89–90)

Frédéric's belief in and awareness of divine providence was a blessing he possessed from youth to his death.

Pause: What place does divine providence hold in your life?

Frédéric's Words

Frédéric used the image of the Gobelin tapestry to reflect his understanding of the workings of providence.

"It is we ourselves . . . who are working out our destiny on earth unknown to us, exactly as the craftsmen of the Gobelins work at their tapestry. Docilely following the design of an unknown artist, they devoted themselves to arranging the several colours indicated by him, on the reverse of the woof, not knowing what the result of their work was to be. It was only afterwards, when the work was completed, that they could admire the flowers, pictures, figures and marvels of art, which then left their hands to adorn the dwellings of kings. Thus, friends, let us work on this earth, docile and submissive to the will of God without knowing what He is accomplishing through us. But He, the divine Artist, sees and knows. When He will show us the finished work of our life, of our toil and of our troubles, we shall then be thrown into ecstasy and we shall bless Him for deigning to accept and place our poor works in His eternal mansion." (Baunard, *Correspondence*, pp. 235–236)

Reflection

Even a cursory reading of Frédéric Ozanam will reveal that divine providence was a major tenet of his life, one of the principal components of his spirituality. Because Frédéric spoke of providence time and time again, the conclusion must be that it was in the forefront of his consciousness. However, like the vast majority of people, Frédéric did not always see God's providence at the time, but he did believe that God's plan was operative everywhere: in the world, in France, in the church, in the Society of Saint Vincent de Paul, and certainly in his own life and family. He understood also the close connection between doing the will of God and recognizing God's providence. Frédéric's frequent references to providence invite us to consider how we interpret the happenings of life in the perspective of faith.

✧ Spend some time with these words of Saint Augustine:

Trust the past to divine mercy,
The present to divine love,
And the future to divine providence.

✧ In what situations are you most aware of the providence of God? Take time to review your life and relive the occasions when the providence of God has been the most manifest. Have some outcomes allowed you to perceive the hand of God? Do some situations await, like the turning of the Gobelin tapestry, a future revelation?

✧ "'We must respect the earth as the workshop of Providence, and our particular employment as the task which has been assigned to us'" (Baunard, *Correspondence,* p. 423).

Responsibility in one's employment and the tasks that belong to it were integral to Frédéric's understanding of doing the will of God within his professional life as a scholar and a teacher. At your place of employment, before your begin your work, ask God for the grace to be responsible to the truth in your professional life.

✧ "'We must respect the earth as the workshop of Providence.'" Today, conservation is a term usually associated with ecology, but conservation also has a spiritual dimension. Divine conservation of our world and of personal human existence is carried out by God's providence. Go outdoors and reflect on your commitment to the preservation of a healthy environment. Make a decision to become involved in a project that shows your respect of the earth.

✧ Take time to consider the relationship between the place of your employment and the conservation of the earth. Ask yourself:

✦ Are there recycling or preservation issues that need to be addressed? Are there personnel policies that need retuning?
✦ Am I in a position that enables me to facilitate changes in policies and procedures?
✦ Do I accept my power and my responsibility to better the situation?

✧ Frédéric comments on the Our Father:

"Our Lord makes us ask in His prayer that His will be done on earth as it is in Heaven. Not as it is in Hell, where it is done of necessity, nor among men, where it is often done with murmuring but as it is in Heaven, with the love and the joy of angels." (Baunard, *Correspondence*, p. 343)

Recite the Our Father with Frédéric's words in mind.

God's Word

He said to his disciples, "Therefore I tell you, do not worry about your life, what you will eat, or about your body, what you will wear. For life is more than food, and the body more than clothing. Consider the ravens: they neither sow nor reap, they have neither storehouse nor barn, and yet God feeds them. Of how much more value are you than the birds! And can any of you by worrying add a single hour to your span of life? If then you are not able to do so small a thing as that, why do you worry about the rest? Consider the lilies, how they grow: they neither toil nor spin; yet I tell you, even Solomon in all his glory was not clothed like one of these. But if God so clothes the grass of the field, which is alive today and tomorrow is thrown into the oven, how much more will he clothe you—you of little faith! And do not keep striving for what you are to eat and what you are to drink, and do not keep worrying. For it is the nations of the world that strive after all these things, and your Father knows that you need them. Instead, strive for his kingdom, and these things will be given to you as well.

"Do not be afraid, little flock, for it is your Father's good pleasure to give you the kingdom." (Luke 12:22–32)

Closing prayer: "Let us go in simplicity where merciful Providence leads us, content to see the stone on which we should step without wanting to discover all at once and completely the windings of the road" (Dirvin, trans. and ed., *Letters*, p. 93).

✧ Meditation 9 ✧

The Weak Samaritan

Theme: Christians are weak Samaritans.

Opening prayer: Compassionate God, grant me the grace to be as compassionate as you are compassionate. May I be as habitually compassionate as Frédéric Ozanam.

About Frédéric

Decorating the wall behind Frédéric Ozanam's tomb in Paris is a fresco by the French artist Rene Dionnet. The painting is that of the good Samaritan. To the left of the tomb, in the fresco, stands a haloed figure holding an unrolled scroll. On the scroll are these words: "Be as the Samaritan of the Gospel. Walk in the charity and example of Christ."

From the time of living in his parent's household to the years of his own maturity, Frédéric understood and lived the parable of the good Samaritan. Even while still young, Frédéric had said of himself, "[I believe that I] am habitually compassionate toward the poor" (Dirvin, trans. and ed., *Letters*, p. 12).

His biographer relates how on one New Year's day he could not help thinking of a poor family who were in reduced circumstances, and had had to pledge some of their furniture, and that when he saw his little girl surrounded with presents he would not rest happy till he had redeemed the furniture and returned it to its owners. On returning from Holy Communion he would frequently visit the baker's shop on his way and purchase bread to distribute among the poor. He had great order in his almsgiving. The budget of his charities was regulated beforehand every year as strictly as any of his personal expenses; and rose in proportion to the increase of his income; he advised all his friends to adopt his plan and thus save themselves the annoyance of never knowing exactly how they stood with regard to this duty, and from saying sometimes "I cannot afford it," without being sure whether they really could or not. (John J. Horgan, *Great Catholic Laymen*, p. 130)

As Frédéric meditated on the parable of the good Samaritan, he began to realize that many of his countrymen, especially the poor, had been robbed of their treasures of faith and love. The ignorance and misconduct that often marked their lives were threads belonging to a larger social fabric. Thus, he wrote:

"God forbid that we should calumniate the poor whom the Gospel blesses, or render the suffering classes responsible for their misery, thus pandering to the hardness of those bad hearts that fancy themselves exonerated from helping the poor man when they have proved his wrongdoing." (O'Meara, *Life and Works*, p. 248)

For Frédéric, then, an essential companion piece to the parable of the good Samaritan was the mandate of Luke 6:37–38: "'Do not judge, and you will not be judged; do not condemn, and you will not be condemned. . . . Give, and it will be given to you.'"

Pause: What habits of compassion and compassionate action have you acquired?

Frédéric's Words

The humanity of our days seems comparable to the traveler of whom the Gospel speaks: it also, although it took its way in roads marked out for it by Christ, has been attacked by the cutthroats and robbers of thought, by wicked men who have robbed it of what it possessed: the treasure of faith and love, and they have left it naked and wounded and lying by the side of the road. Priests and levites have passed by, and this time, since they were true priests and levites, they have approached suffering themselves and wished to heal it. But in its delirium, it did not recognize them and repulsed them.

In our turn, weak Samaritans, worldly and people of little faith that we are, let us dare nonetheless to approach this great sick one. Perhaps it will not be frightened of us. Let us try to probe its wounds and pour in oil, soothing its ear with words of consolation and peace; then, when its eyes are opened, we will place it in the hands of those whom God has constituted as the guardians and doctors of souls, who are also, in a way, our innkeepers in our pilgrimage here below, so as to give our errant and famished spirits the holy word for nourishment and the hope of a better world for a shield. (Dirvin, trans. and ed., *Letters*, pp. 64–65)

Reflection

Compassion is a combination of two Latin words meaning "to suffer with." Compassion means entering into the suffering and pain of others who have been victimized on the same road we travel. It means doing what we can to alleviate the immediate suffering and pain and then making the appropriate provisions for long-term care and healing. Compassion allows us to feel and understand the plight of the victimized. Their experience is not outside our personal reality. Compassion includes personal presence, hands-on assistance, and heartfelt concern. Frédéric developed the compassion he learned from his parents by meditation on the Scriptures and by his own involvement with the poor. He challenges us to do the same.

✧ Frédéric does not call Christians "good Samaritans," as one would expect, but "weak Samaritans." We are indeed weak human beings who attend to other weak human beings by acts of compassion. Would you prefer to be called a good Samaritan rather than a weak Samaritan? If so, why? Ask yourself some further questions:

✦ What is it that motivates your acts of compassion?
✦ Can you transcend apathy and prejudice in helping others?
✦ Do you see humanity in general as a victim robbed of faith and love?
✦ Have you developed habits of compassion?

✧ Meditatively read the "Frédéric's Words" section again. Spend time listening to Frédéric speaking these words to you. When you come across a phrase or a word that especially touches your heart, talk about that phrase or word with Frédéric. Ask him what he meant by it. When you have finished your dialog, write down some of your reflections on Frédéric's words.

✧ Read the "God's Word" section that follows. In a period of five days, imagine the event on the road to Jericho in which you are, alternately: the beaten and robbed traveler, the robber, the priest or Levite, the Samaritan, and finally, the innkeeper.

✦ In each case recreate the scenario, let the events and your actions unfold, and stay in touch with the various feelings aroused.
✦ Journal about your experience as each figure.
✦ Conclude each journaling session with a petitionary prayer.

✧ Traditionally in the church, many have seen the good Samaritan as the Christ symbol. But another way of looking at it is to see the victim at the side of the road as the Christ symbol. The victim is the one who is affecting people's lives, who is causing people to make decisions. The Christ symbol, half-dead and powerless, stirs the conscience and forces decisions on those who are traveling along the same route—to be compassionate or not.

Recall when others reached out in compassion to you. When were you the victim, the poor one, the sick one, the abandoned one?

✧ Martin Luther King Jr. is quoted as saying that love is not satisfied with comforting those who suffer,

> "We must be the good Samaritan to those who have fallen along the way. This, however, is only the beginning. Then, some day we will necessarily have to realize that the road to Jericho must be made in such a way that men and women are not constantly beaten and robbed while they are going along the paths of life." (*Christian Community Bible*, 2nd ed., p. 161)

Create a dialog between Frédéric Ozanam and Martin Luther King Jr. in which they talk about the perils of their times, the treasures that have been stolen, the identities of the victims and the robbers, what the Samaritans traveling along the same road as the victim need to do to show compassion, and how the Jericho road can be remade so that those who travel will no longer be beaten and robbed. Share this dialog with friends or with a group that you belong to. Perform it as a neighborhood or parish one-act play.

God's Word

[The lawyer,] wanting to justify himself, . . . asked Jesus, "And who is my neighbor?" Jesus replied, "A man was going down from Jerusalem to Jericho and fell into the hands of robbers, who stripped him, beat him, and went away, leaving him half dead. Now by chance a priest was going down the road; and when he saw him, he passed by on the other side. So likewise a Levite, when he came to the place and saw him, passed by on the other side. But a Samaritan while traveling came near him; and when he saw him, he was moved with pity. He went to him and bandaged his wounds, having poured oil and wine on them. Then he put him on his own animal,

brought him to an inn, and took care of him. The next day
he took out two denarii, gave them to the innkeeper, and
said, 'Take care of him; and when I come back, I will repay you whatever more you spend.' Which of these three,
do you think, was a neighbor to the man who fell into the
hands of the robbers?" He said, "The one who showed
him mercy." Jesus said to him, "Go and do likewise."
(Luke 10:29–37)

Closing prayer: O loving and gracious God, thank you
for your compassion to me. Thank you for the countless times
when you stooped down to soothe me and care for me. Grant
me the grace to be a person of compassion to others, regard-
less of who they may be, family, friend, or stranger.

Forming a Network of Charity

Theme: "'Let us go to the poor'" (Baunard, *Correspondence*, p. 65).

Opening prayer: Jesus, messiah of the poor, you said that the poor are always with us. Grant us the grace to love the poor and poverty as Frédéric Ozanam did.

About Frédéric

In God's providence, a fellow student who was a devotee of the theories of Saint-Simon launched Frédéric Ozanam's ministry to the poor. This peer challenged Frédéric with these thoughts:

> "Today Christianity is dead. Indeed, you people who boast about being Catholics, what are you doing? Where are the works which demonstrate your Faith and which can make you respected and accepted?" (Austin Fagan, *Through the Eye of a Needle*, p. 205)

At a meeting with six others on a Tuesday night in April 1833, the Holy Spirit inspired Frédéric with these words that touched the heart and mind of each person in the room:

"We must do what is most agreeable to God. Therefore, we must do what our Lord Jesus Christ did when preaching the Gospel. Let us go to the poor." (Baunard, *Correspondence*, p. 65)

M. Bailly had the following words of advice and encouragement for the young men:

"Most of you are studying to be lawyers, . . . some to be doctors; . . . go and help the poor, each in your special line; let your studies be of use to others as well as to yourselves; it is a good and easy way of commencing your apostolate as Christians in the world.
  "If you intend the work to be really efficacious, . . . if you are in earnest about serving the poor as well as yourselves, you must not let it be a mere doling out of alms, bringing each your pittance of money or food; you must make it a medium of moral assistance, you must give them the alms of good advice." (O'Meara, *Life and Works*, pp. 62, 61)

Then and there was founded the Conference of Charity whose name was changed on 4 February 1834 to the Society of Saint Vincent de Paul. From that time on, Frédéric Ozanam would never be the same; the poor were always with him.

Pause: What part do the poor play in your life?

Frédéric's Words

In his book *The Franciscan Poets in Italy of the Thirteenth Century*, Frédéric spoke of Saint Francis of Assisi:

In becoming poor, in founding a new order of poor men like himself, he honoured Poverty, which is the most despised and the most universal of human conditions. He showed that in such a state may be found peace, dignity, and happiness. By so doing he pacified the resentful feelings of the indigent classes, reconciled them to the rich whom they learnt to envy no more. He made a truce in that ancient war between those who have and those who have not, and strengthened the bonds already loosened of Christian society.

By so doing, this mad man proved that he possessed the greatest possible tact, and that he had had reason to foresee that he would become a great prince; for whereas Plato never found fifty families to realise his ideal republic, the servant of God at the end of eleven years numbered a following of five thousand men, busied like himself in a life of heroism and strife. But this life, hard beyond conception, was also the freest, and, in consequence, the most poetic. Indeed, one thing alone confines human liberty, namely fear, and all fear becoming ultimately the fear of suffering could have no weight with one who regarded suffering as a joy and glory. (Pp. 68–69)

Reflection

Frédéric had a high sensitivity to the poor and to poverty. He held a preferential option for the poor in his life as did his patron, Saint Vincent de Paul, long before the term became operative in theology. The poor meant more than the "financially disadvantaged." While dedicating his life to the service of truth, Frédéric perceived that he was affirming truth when he showed the vitality of his faith in good works toward the poor. Frédéric's decision "to go to the poor" was made with others of like mind and intent. He desired to form a network of charity. This network spread itself throughout France, its neighboring countries, and beyond.

A vivid example of Frédéric's preference for the poor took place in London. He, his wife, and friend J. J. Ampère had traveled to London in August 1851 to see the Crystal Palace exhibition. Frédéric left them at the exhibition while he went to visit the poor Irish Catholics who lived in the tenements located on the streets surrounding the hall. When Frédéric returned, his wife and friend found him deeply moved by the plight of *la misère* and somewhat poorer than when he left them. He sat down and shared this experience with them.

✧ Frédéric responded to the call of his faith, as found in the Scriptures:

> What good is it, my brothers and sisters, if you say you have faith but do not have works? Can faith save you? If a brother or sister is naked and lacks daily food, and one of you says to them, "Go in peace; keep warm and eat your fill," and yet you do not supply their bodily needs, what is the good of that? So faith by itself, if it has no works, is dead. (James 2:14–16)

What are you doing for those in need in your world? Volunteer at a local food pantry, soup kitchen, thrift store, Vincent de Paul center, or Catholic Worker house.

✧ Reread the "Frédéric's Words" section. Knowing what you know about poverty and the poor, do you agree with Frédéric's insights? Is fear the one thing that confines human liberty? Does fear now confine your liberty? Name that fear.

✧ Take time to pray about the feelings of the rich toward the poor and of the poor toward the rich that Frédéric mentioned, that is, envy, resentment, and so on. Add your own words to these lists. What can be done for either group to change these feelings. Pray for the gifts of tact and freedom for those called to mediate between rich people and poor people.

✧ Pope John Paul II states in his apostolic letter "Tertio Millennio Adveniente":

> If we recall that Jesus came to "preach the good news to the poor" (Mt. 11:5; Lk. 7:22), how can we fail to lay greater emphasis on the church's preferential option for the poor and the outcast? (*Origins*, 24 November 1994, p. 414)

What does the phrase "preferential option for the poor" mean to you? How would you rank your own sensitivity to poor people on a scale of one to ten? Describe your sensitivity by way of imagery. Pray for greater compassion.

God's Word

For you know the generous act of our Lord Jesus Christ, that though he was rich, yet for your sakes he became poor, so that by his poverty you might become rich. (2 Corinthians 8:9)

Closing prayer: Jesus, messiah of the poor, may we be carriers of your good news to the poor—to those who lack resources, who lack options, who lack power over their own life. May we help the poor by acts of compassion that alleviate their needs and give them hope.

✧ **Meditation 11** ✧

Blessed Are the Merciful

Theme: "'Blessed are the merciful, for they will receive mercy'" (Matthew 5:7).

Opening prayer: Merciful God, be merciful to me, a sinner. May I in turn show your mercy to others in word and deed.

About Frédéric

The Society of Saint Vincent de Paul started off as a small group.

> The rules of the Society were simple but stringent. It was forbidden to discuss politics or personal concerns at the meetings; . . . the Society was never to be made use of as a stepping-stone to worldly advancement. This clause, which was emphatically expressed, seemed rather superfluous, considering how remote the chances were of the members being in a position to violate it; but it was inserted as a counterpart to [the Conference of Good Studies] on which the historical conferences were in a certain sense grafted, and whose members were pledged to help each other on in the world. Nothing of the sort was to be tolerated in the new confraternity; no selfish principle was to inspire its action; it was to be animated only by

charity, by love of God and of suffering humanity, without any kind of reference to self. The same spirit was to preside at the weekly conferences; there was to be no display of eloquence or learning, nothing but the reports of the week summed up in a businesslike manner, and the interests of the poor discussed in brief and simple language. (O'Meara, *Life and Works*, p. 63)

One of the first cases Frédéric resolved as a member of the Society involved a woman and her five children who were consistently physically abused by her live-in partner. Any money the destitute mother made was confiscated by the alcoholic father. When Frédéric found her, she had reached the end of her rope. As a person of deep compassion and with legal expertise, Frédéric convinced the woman that, in reality, she had no legal or moral obligation to remain in such a relationship. There never had been any form of marriage. She and the children should escape this situation in which they were objects of such abusive behavior. Frédéric collected money and assisted the woman in relocation to another part of France where she could begin a new life. Her two eldest children came under the employment of M. Bailly, assisting at the printing office and residing in his home. This family was very grateful for Frédéric's assistance.

Frédéric heard the call of Jesus—to be merciful. He saw the works of mercy as calls to action. He believed that if he genuinely wanted to serve the poor and others, he had to direct his works of mercy to the moral and spiritual betterment of individuals, not only to the alleviation of their physical distress.

Pause: Can you say that one of your attitudes is that of being merciful?

Frédéric's Words

On 21 October 1848, Frédéric wrote a remarkable article in his newspaper, the *New Era*. The article was entitled "Help Which Humiliates and Help Which Honors."

"Help is humiliating when it appeals to men from below, taking heed of their material wants only, paying no attention but to those of the flesh, to the cry of hunger and cold, to what excites pity, to what one succors even in the beasts. It humiliates when there is no reciprocity, when you give the poor man nothing but bread, or clothes, or a bundle of straw—what, in fact, there is no likelihood of his ever giving you in return. . . . But it honors when it appeals to him from above, when it occupies itself with his soul, his religious, moral, and political education, with all that emancipates him from his passions and from a portion of his wants, with those things that make him free, and may make him great. Help honors when to the bread that nourishes it adds the visit that consoles, the advice that enlightens, the friendly shake of the hand that lifts up the sinking courage; when it treats the poor man with respect, not only as an equal but as a superior, since he is suffering what perhaps we are incapable of suffering; since he is the messenger of God to us, sent to prove our justice and our charity, and to save us by our works.

"Help then becomes honorable, because it may become mutual, because every man who gives a kind word, a good advice, a consolation today, may tomorrow stand himself in need of a kind word, an advice, or a consolation; because the hand that you clasp clasps yours in return; because that indigent family whom you love loves you in return, and will have largely acquitted themselves towards you when the old man, the mother, the little children shall have prayed for you." (O'Meara, *Life and Works*, pp. 176–177)

Reflection

Jesus Christ taught that [a person] not only receives and experiences the mercy of God, but that each is also called "to practice mercy" toward others: "Blessed are the merciful, for they shall obtain mercy" (Matthew 5:7). The church sees in these words a call to action, and she tries to practice mercy. (*Rich in Mercy Encyclical*, no. 14, p. 44)

For Frédéric, the beatitudes were attitudes of being and doing; they were the axis around which his entire Christian life revolved. Frédéric makes a distinction between philanthropy and charity.

> Philanthropy is a vain woman for whom good actions are a piece of jewelry and who loves to look at herself in the mirror. Charity is a tender mother who keeps her eyes fixed on the infant she carries at her breast, who no longer thinks of herself, and who forgets her beauty for her love. (Dirvin, trans. and ed., *Letters*, p. 63)

His words may seem strong, but for his time and culture they were most probably very accurate. Frédéric invites us to examine not only what we do on behalf of others, but also the attitudes that motivate us.

✧ What do you think of Frédéric's distinction between philanthropy and charity? Reflect on the similarities and differences in their practice today by posing the following questions:

+ What are the motivations for philanthropy? What are the motivations for practicing the works of mercy?
+ What is given in philanthropy? What is given in practicing the works of mercy?
+ What are the expectations of return for those who practice philanthropy? For those who practice the works of mercy?

Close with a prayer that remembers both those who practice philanthropy and those who practice the works of mercy.

✧ In the *Merchant of Venice,* William Shakespeare writes:

> The quality of mercy is not strained. It droppeth as the gentle rain from heaven upon the place beneath. It is twice blest: it blesseth him that gives and him that takes. 'Tis mightiest in the mightiest. . . . [Mercy] is an attribute to God himself. And earthly power doth then show likest God's when mercy seasons justice. (Act 4, scene 1)

Do you see any connection between Shakespeare's words here and Frédéric's attitude and manner?

✧ Identify one area of your life that could be simplified to free some of your time, talent, or money for merciful service to your neighbor. Take action; make specific plans. Take your time and talent and share it cordially with lonely, sick, imprisoned, or homebound people.

✧ Frédéric advises the Society of Saint Vincent de Paul:

"Sons of Saint Vincent de Paul, let us learn of Him to forget ourselves, to devote ourselves to the service of God and the good of men. Let us learn of Him that holy preference which shows most love to those who suffer most." (Baunard, *Correspondence*, p. 273)

Should our acts of mercy be so directed to those who suffer most? What would this mean for you?

God's Word

"Blessed are the poor in spirit, for theirs is the kingdom of heaven.

"Blessed are those who mourn, for they will be comforted.

"Blessed are the meek, for they will inherit the earth.

"Blessed are those who hunger and thirst for righteousness, for they will be filled.

"Blessed are the merciful, for they will receive mercy.

"Blessed are the pure in heart, for they will see God.

"Blessed are the peacemakers, for they will be called children of God.

"Blessed are those who are persecuted for righteousness' sake, for theirs is the kingdom of heaven." (Matthew 5:3–10)

Closing prayer: Merciful and loving God, may I see my acts of mercy as truly your call to action. May I direct my works of mercy to moral and spiritual betterment and not merely to physical alleviation of my neighbors' needs.

Practicing the Works of Mercy

Theme: The works of mercy are our response in compassion to those who suffer in body, mind, and spirit. These persons are, in truth, Jesus to us.

Opening prayer: Jesus, crucified and risen, grant me the grace to see your face in the faces of my suffering brothers and sisters.

About Frédéric

"You have amongst your children many who are rich, Reverend Father—oh! what a salutary lesson, how strengthening for those soft young hearts, to show them the poor, to show them Jesus Christ, not in pictures painted by great masters or on altars resplendent with gold and light, but to show them Jesus Christ and His wounds in the persons of the poor!" (O'Meara, *Life and Works*, p. 335)

Thus did Frédéric write Father Pendola of Tuscany who had just started a Conference of the Society of Saint Vincent de Paul. Frédéric desired that the young be introduced to the living reality of Christ in the world.

Although Frédéric himself had the advantage of exemplary parents to show the reality of the Christian life and faith and the fraternal support of the newly founded Society of Saint Vincent de Paul, he knew the world he lived in was becoming ever more materialistic, antagonistic, and prone to despair.

It was not long before Frédéric and the other members of the Society of Saint Vincent de Paul, in their attempt to combine the corporal and spiritual works of mercy as they reached out to the poor, met not only grateful response but also, at times, indifference and coldness. After their first two years of ministry, Frédéric wrote:

> Our poor are cold and despairingly indifferent. They have natures used to material civilization, which are no longer disposed to take to religion, which no longer have a sense of invisible things, which hold out their hands to receive bread, but whose ears remain forever closed to the word we proclaim to them. (Dirvin, trans. and ed., *Letters*, p. 71)

Their spirits had become dull and hard—a characteristic that led Frédéric, however, to regard them as the most wounded poor. They were never outside the mercy of God and Frédéric's continuing concern. About the culture surrounding everyone, Frédéric remarked, "'I am quite disenchanted by the monotonous uniformity in which material civilization threatens to envelop the whole world'" (O'Meara, *Life and Works*, p. 265).

The conditions of distressing misery of the poor of Paris—crowded quarters, the lack of a sewer system, the dirt, the rats—were not outside Frédéric's experience. These seared his heart and bound it closer together with that of the wounded Christ. The practice of the works of mercy was the active homage Frédéric paid to his master.

Pause: When you do a work of mercy for someone—friend or stranger—whom do you see in the face of that person?

Frédéric's Words

Both men and the poor we see with the eyes of the flesh; they are there and we can put finger and hand in their wounds and the scars of the crown of thorns are visible on their foreheads; and at this point incredulity no longer has place and we should fall at their feet and say with the Apostle, *Tu est Dominus et Deus meus.* You are our masters, and we will be your servants. You are for us the sacred images of that God whom we do not see, and not knowing how to love Him otherwise shall we not love Him in your persons? (Dirvin, trans. and ed., *Letters*, p. 96)

Reflection

The essence of Frédéric's spirituality, which is mainly Vincentian spirituality, is the identification of Christ with the poor. The scriptural foundation for this is the last judgment scene as described by Jesus in Matthew 25:31–46. Here Jesus specifies the works of mercy and identifies himself with the person who is hungry, homeless, naked, sick, imprisoned. "As you did it to one of the least of these who are members of my family, you did it to me'" (Matthew 25:40).

Frédéric responds to Jesus' identification with the poor, but he also has another scriptural image and narrative that informs him: the risen Jesus showing his wounds to the Apostle Thomas as found in John 20:24–28. It is the risen Jesus whose scars and nailprints the poor and suffering bear on their bodies, and it is with the eyes of faith as well as the eyes of the flesh that Frédéric sees this.

✧ Reread the "Frédéric's Words" section. Frédéric is sharing with us how he understands both the mystery of the risen Jesus and his identification with the wounded poor. Read John 20:24–28. Enter into the astonishment and humility of Thomas. Be reverent when you next approach someone who is obviously wounded. Pray to see, like Frédéric, the risen Christ in the person of the poor.

✧ Frédéric said that the poor are often cold and despairingly indifferent. He was struggling with a characteristic of his age and time. Reread Frédéric's words found in the passage above. Where do you find indifference and hopelessness in the world today? How can these wounds be healed? Pray for patience and perseverance for yourself and for those who in their concerned commitment most need it.

✧ Of the fourteen traditional works of mercy, which of them do you practice the most? The least? Wherein are your gifts and skills?

The Corporal Works of Mercy
To feed the hungry
To give drink to the thirsty
To clothe the naked
To visit those in prison
To shelter the homeless
To visit the sick
To bury the dead

The Spiritual Works of Mercy
To admonish the sinner
To instruct the ignorant
To counsel the doubtful
To comfort the sorrowful
To bear wrongs patiently
To forgive all injuries
To pray for the living and dead

God's Word

"When the Son of Man comes in his glory, and all the angels with him, then he will sit on the throne of his glory. All the nations will be gathered before him, and he will separate people one from another as a shepherd separates the sheep from the goats, and he will put the sheep at his right hand and the goats at the left. Then the king will say to those at his right hand, 'Come you that are blessed by my Father, inherit the kingdom prepared for you from the foundation of the world; for I was hungry and you gave me food, I was thirsty and you gave me something to drink, I was a stranger and you welcomed me, I was naked and you gave me clothing, I was sick and you took care of me, I was in prison and you visited me.' Then the righteous will answer him, 'Lord, when was it that we saw you hungry and gave you food, or thirsty and gave you something to drink? And when was it that we saw you a stranger and welcomed you, or naked and gave you clothing? And when was it that we saw you sick or in prison and visited you?' And the king will answer them, 'Truly I tell you, just as you did it to one of the least of these who are members of my family, you did it to me.' Then he will say to those at his left hand, 'You that are accursed, depart from me into the eternal fire prepared for the devil and his angels; for I was hungry and you gave me no food, I was thirsty and you gave me nothing to drink, I was a stranger and you did not welcome me, naked and you did not give me clothing, sick and in prison and you did not visit me.' Then they also will answer, 'Lord, when was it that we saw you hungry or thirsty or a stranger or naked or sick or in prison, and did not take care of you?' Then he will answer them, 'Truly I tell you, just as you did not do it to one of the least of these, you did not do it to me.' And these will go away into eternal punishment, but the righteous into eternal life." (Matthew 25:31–46)

Closing prayer: Jesus, crucified and risen, grant me the grace to be ever more compassionate as I behold your wounds in the wounded poor. Give me the gift of an understanding heart. Grant me the grace to see you in the faces of my fellow human beings, especially in the faces of the poor, sick, lonely, and abandoned.

Martyrdom

Theme: A martyr is a witness to the faith. This witnessing takes various forms with diverse consequences.

Opening prayer: O loving God, may I be a credible witness in my life to the faith that you have given me.

About Frédéric

Frédéric Ozanam was more than familiar with martyrs and martyrdom. His ancestors were converted from Judaism to Catholicism by Saint Didier, a martyr. The Ozanams saw religious and priests martyred during French revolutionary periods. Frédéric grew up in the city of Lyon, a city of martyrs, a place where Christians had been put to death by the Romans in the second century.

During his life in Paris, Frédéric attended Mass at a church that was next to the site of the massacre of 114 priests. As a layman in the first half of the nineteenth century, in an environment hostile to Christianity, Frédéric witnessed others whose blood was shed for the faith, most notably the Paris archbishop Affre, who lost his life in an effort to reconcile opposing forces in the 1848 civil uprising.

Martyrdom seems to have always been in the back of Frédéric's mind because he spoke of it frequently. In a conference with others of the academy, Frédéric spoke with heartfelt ardor:

> "Gentlemen, day by day, our friends, our brothers, are killed as soldiers in Africa or as missionaries in the land of the Mandarins. What are we doing the while? Can you believe that God has assigned to some the duty of dying in the service of civilisation and of the Church, and to others that of standing idly by or reclining on a bed of roses? Ah! Gentlemen, as Christian workers in the fields of Science and of Literature, let us prove that we are not so cowardly as to believe in such an allocation of duties, as would be an accusation against the God Who would have made it, and a shame for us who would have accepted it. Let us be prepared to prove that, we too, have our fields of battle on which we know how to die." (Baunard, *Correspondence*, pp. 236–237)

The fields of battle for Frédéric Ozanam were not only the arenas of the poor, but also the milieus of the young whom he served at the university. In the winter of 1852, Ozanam had faithfully delivered the courses for the session even as illness was sapping his strength. In the spring he was confined to bed in great pain and with a high fever. However,

> one day he heard that the public were clamoring for him at the Sorbonne, accusing him of self-indulgence and neglect of duty in being so long absent from his [course], when he was paid by the State for giving it. The news stung him to the quick. "I will show them it is not true. I will do honor to my profession!" (O'Meara, *Life and Works*, p. 275)

Against the entreaties of his wife, his brother, and a medical attendant, Frédéric got dressed and drove to the university. Wan and weak, he leaned on the arm of a friend as he entered the premises. When finally placed before the young men, he said to them clearly and straightforwardly:

> "Gentlemen, . . . our age is accused of being an age of egotism; we professors, it is said, are tainted with the general epidemic; and yet it is here that we use up our health;

it is here that we wear ourselves out. I do not complain of it; our life belongs to you; we owe it to you to our last breath, and you shall have it. For my part, if I die it will be in your service!" (O'Meara, *Life and Works*, p. 276)

Ozanam continued his lecture with the eloquence and force that had become his trademark. However, after this day he was never strong enough to return to the classroom or the podium. His witness given in this forum ended forever.

Pause: Do you ever think about martyrdom? In what forum do you "give" your life?

Frédéric's Words

"The world has grown cold, it is for us Catholics to rekindle the vital fire which had been extinguished. It is for us to inaugurate the era of the martyrs, for it is a martyrdom possible to every Christian. To give one's life for God and for one's brothers [and sisters], to give one's life in sacrifice, is to be a martyr. It is indifferent whether the sacrifice be consummated at one moment, or whether slowly consuming, it fills the altar night and day with sweet perfume. To be a martyr is to give back to heaven all that one has received, wealth, life, our whole soul. It is in our power to make this offering, this sacrifice. It is for us to select the altar at which we shall dedicate it; the divinity to whom we shall consecrate youth and life; the temple where we shall meet again: at the feet of the idol of egotism, or in the sanctuary of God and Humanity." (Baunard, *Correspondence*, p. 97)

Reflection

In the document "Tertio Millennio Adveniente," Pope John Paul II calls for an updating of the martyrology, a written memorial naming those who have given their life for the faith. These include not only . . . those who have shed their blood for Christ but also . . . teachers of the faith, missionaries, confessors, bishops, priests, virgins, married couples, widows and children.

. . . The greatest homage which all the churches can give to Christ on the threshold of the third millennium will be to manifest the redeemer's all-powerful presence through the fruits of faith, hope and charity present in men and women of many different tongues and races who have followed Christ in the various forms of the Christian vocation. (*Origins*, 24 November 1994, pp. 411–412)

All are called to remember those who have given their life in martyrdom and to be mindful of the various forms martyrdom has taken.

❖ All martyrs are distinguished by generosity. There are many ways to be generous. Use the following passage by Lord Balfour as an examination of conscience. Add five of your own thoughts to this litany:

The best thing to give your enemy is forgiveness
to an opponent, tolerance
to a friend, your heart
to your child, a good example
to a father, deference
to your mother, conduct that will make her proud of you
to yourself, respect
to all men [and women], charity.

❖ Light a candle or set a fire in a fireplace if you have one. Reread the "Frédéric's Words" section, pausing on the sentences or phrases that are significant for you. If you have a hard time focusing your attention, write out this passage slowly on good paper. What form has martyrdom taken for you? What form has it taken for those persons who are dear to you? Have you ever noticed its "sweet perfume"? Have you selected the altar on which to dedicate this sacrifice? Do you approach this altar with reverence?

When you have finished this meditation, take a period of time to gaze at the flame and to feel the warmth of the fire. Close with a prayer of thanksgiving and dedication.

✧ "The blood of martyrs is the seed of Christianity" (cf. *Origins*, 24 November 1994, pp. 411, 416). Meditate on this phrase, word by word, letting each one resonate within you. Think of the martyrs you know about who have lived in the twentieth century. Ask the Spirit to come to your aid in guiding your mind and heart. After a time of reflection, write in your journal the thoughts that come to you in this meditation. Return to this thought the next day, and repeat the reflection and the writing exercise. As a conclusion to these two days of prayer, design a small logo signifying martyrdom to place at the end of the journal page.

✧ Think of a dimension of your faith that is most difficult for you. Write it down at the top of a page of paper. Plan to make a pilgrimage to a cemetery, a church, or a shrine where martyrs can be honored. When you make this pilgrimage, pray in anticipation for this gift of faith. When you have arrived, pray ardently for this gift. Before you depart, write a prayer of thanksgiving on the paper as if you had already received this gift.

God's Word

Jesus told his disciples, "If any want to become my followers, let them deny themselves and take up their cross and follow me. For those who want to save their life will lose it, and those who lose their life for my sake will find it. For what will it profit them if they gain the whole world but forfeit their life? Or what will they give in return for their life?" (Matthew 16:24–26)

Closing prayer: O holy God, the deaths of your martyrs reveal your power shining through our human weakness. You choose the weak and make them strong in being witnesses for you. Give me the altar, the sanctuary, the temple where I can offer this pleasing sacrifice of my life to you.

✧ Meditation 14 ✧

Suffering

Theme: Christians accept their suffering with love in union with the sufferings of Jesus.

Opening prayer: "'O my God! I thank Thee for the afflictions and the sufferings Thou have sent me in this place; accept them in expiation of my sins.'" (O'Meara, *Life and Works*, p. 344).

About Frédéric

Frédéric Ozanam's fragile health was his daily cross, a "gospel of suffering" from his youth. Throughout the decades of his short life, Frédéric would easily become fatigued. He was intelligent enough to know that he needed a doctor's expertise, but not always prudent enough to slow down the pace of his daily life. He kept himself on an intensely active and demanding schedule. The passion of his spirit did not always match the capacities of his body.

A year before he died, he wrote to a friend concerning his sufferings and his petitions to God: "'Let Him only give me courage and send me the suffering that purifies. May my cross be that of the penitent thief'" (Baunard, *Correspondence*, p. 364).

During this last year of his life, Frédéric was excessively debilitated. "'I am a prey to a long and grievous malady, which is the more dangerous that it hides perhaps a complete exhaustion'" (Frédéric Ozanam, *Bible of the Sick*, p. 15).

Reading the sacred Scriptures was Frédéric's consolation in suffering. Every day he would read the word of God and underline passages that spoke to his heart. He wrote:

"During many weeks of extreme languor the Psalms have never been out of my hands. I was never wearied of reading over and over those sublime lamentations, those flights of hope, those supplications of full love which answer to all the wants and all the miseries of human nature." (Ozanam, *Bible of the Sick*, p. 13)

Frédéric's biographer wrote of him:

He derived such extraordinary comfort and sustenance from this practice, that it occurred to him he might in his helplessness still render a last service to other invalids by pointing out to them the passages that had soothed and nourished his own soul in the course of his illness. His wife gladly acquiesced in the suggestion, and every morning wrote down some pages from his dictation. (O'Meara, *Life and Works*, p. 330)

These writings were subsequently published with the title *The Bible of the Sick*.

Pause: How do you respond to suffering? Is it an invitation to more tender and intelligent care?

Frédéric's Words

"I come, if Thou callest me, and I have no right to complain. Thou hast given forty years of life to a creature who entered this world sickly, fragile, destined to die ten times, if ten times he had not been rescued by the tenderness and intelligence of a father and mother. Let not my people be scandalized if thou dost not see good now to work a miracle in order to save me! . . . Five years ago Thou didst bring me back almost from death, and was not this delay granted me to do penance and become better? Ah! the prayers that were sent up to Thee then were heard. Why should those that are being offered now, and in so far greater number, on my behalf, be lost? Perhaps Thou wilt answer them, Lord, in another way. Thou wilt give me courage, resignation, peace of soul, and those ineffable consolations that accompany Thy real presence. Thou wilt enable me to find in illness a source of merit and of blessings, and these blessings Thou wilt cause to fall on my wife and my child—on all those to whom my labors perchance would have been less useful than my sufferings. If I express the years of my life with bitterness before Thee, it is because of the sins that have sullied them; but when I consider the graces that have enriched them, I look back upon them, Lord, with gratitude to Thee.

"If Thou shouldst chain me to this sick-bed for the days that I have yet to live, they would be too short to thank Thee for the days that I have lived. Ah! if these pages be the last that I ever write, may they be a hymn to Thy goodness!" (Ozanam, *Bible of the Sick*, pp. 16–17)

Reflection

Frédéric called his wife, Amélie, his guardian angel because she was ever at his side caring for him and responding to his needs. In his attempt to enter into a spirit of gratitude for his life, he said to Amélie, "'I want you also to praise and bless God for our sufferings. . . . I bless Him for all the consolation which you have given me'" (Baunard, *Correspondence*, p. 402).

The manner in which Frédéric accepted his illness invites us to reflect on the chronic situations of our health, the faith and petitions we bring to times of suffering, and the way we respond to those around us who are caring for us.

✧ Do an examination of consciousness on your response to sickness and suffering.

✦ What effect has suffering had on you?

✦ Do you turn inward?

✦ Do you become bitter?

✦ Can you communicate your feelings?

✦ Do you allow others to practice charity toward you?

✦ Do you see your spouse, your friend, or a nurse as a guardian angel?

✦ Do you thank them in some way?

✧ Quiet and center yourself. In your imagination, picture a multitude of the sick—the sick of this world or the sick in your local area. Imagine them in beds and cots under a blue sky. They are present before you, but helpless and speechless. Open your Bible to the Book of Psalms, and begin to pray the Psalms for these sick who are present before you. Cry out in their name; sing praises in their name. Stay with any psalm or moment of silence that awakens the spirit of serenity or awe. When you are finished, recite a blessing with raised hands over all the sick before you. Gently bring yourself back to the room you are in.

✧ The penitent thief's words to Jesus were, "'Jesus, remember me when you come into your kingdom.'" Go for a half-hour walk, reciting these words as a refrain or chant. Allow your current thoughts and feelings to surface. Continue to savor the words; let them enter deeper within you. During the day, recall the words "'Jesus, remember me.'"

✧ Spend some time listing your physical and moral sufferings. Which causes the most pain? What graces have you learned to expect from them? Reread the "Frédéric's Words" section and ask for the virtues you need to reconcile yourself with them.

God's Word

One of the criminals who were hanged there kept deriding him and saying, "Are you not the Messiah? Save yourself and us!" But the other rebuked him, saying, "Do you not fear God, since you are under the same sentence of condemnation? And we indeed have been condemned justly, for we are getting what we deserve for our deeds, but this man has done nothing wrong." Then he said,

"Jesus, remember me when you come into your kingdom." He replied, "Truly I tell you, today you will be with me in Paradise." (Luke 23:39–43)

Closing prayer:

In the splendor of his rising, Christ conquered suffering and death and gave to us the promise of a new and glorious world where no bodily pain will afflict us and no anguish of spirit will harm us. Through your gift of the Spirit, you bless us, even now, with comfort and healing, strength and hope, forgiveness and peace. (Adapted from *Rites of the Catholic Church*, vol. 1, no. 145, pp. 836–837)

✧ Meditation 15 ✧

Meeting Death

Theme: Peace of heart allows us to bear the hardest trials and the approach of death.

Opening prayer: "'My God, my God, have mercy on me'" Baunard, *Correspondence*, p. 403.

About Frédéric

Six months before he died, Frédéric shared these insights with a friend:

> "What better preparation for death than a long sickness and plenty of good works? When I see Christians tried by long and cruel suffering, I picture to myself souls making their Purgatory in this world, and worthy of the respectful pity we owe to the just in the Church suffering. (Ozanam, *Bible of the Sick*, p. 11)

Frédéric himself obviously had led a life of good works and, in the last year of his life, had suffered from very poor health. Although he was generally weak, he had periods of increased well-being.

In 1852, he and his family went to Italy. There they enjoyed the soft warmth of the Italian summer. "I take long walks," Frédéric wrote to his friend Ampère,

"I pass my morning on the rocks, watching the sea, until I have learned the play of its waves by heart. I am gaining strength but slowly, which was to be expected after so severe a crisis." (O'Meara, *Life and Works*, pp. 333–334)

As the days and weeks passed, Frédéric pondered the great mystery that lay ahead of him. He spoke frequently of his sins, of the punishment they deserved, of the scandal they caused, and of the responsibilities of Catholics. When a friend tried to soothe him with more consoling thoughts, Frédéric replied, "'Child, you do not know what the sanctity of God is!'" (O'Meara, *Life and Works*, p. 342).

His last days were described this way:

"He lived almost out of doors, stretched on his sofa, which had been wheeled out to the terrace, and there he would lie silent for hours with the Bible open by his side. One evening he lay thus, watching the sun sinking into the blue Mediterranean; his wife had drawn her chair a little behind him, . . . when something in the extreme serenity of his countenance prompted her to ask which of all the gifts of God he considered the greatest. He replied without hesitating, . . . '*Peace of heart;* without this we may possess everything and yet not be happy; with it we can bear the hardest trials and the approach of death.'" (O'Meara, *Life and Works*, p. 343)

From this time on, Frédéric seemed to possess this peace of heart.

Not long after, conscious of Frédéric's failing health, the Ozanams returned to France. Upon landing at Marseilles, they were met at the dock by Amélie's mother and other members of her family. Frédéric said to them:

"Behold one journey completed; I shall make another, but I shall make it in tranquillity. Now that I have placed Amélie in your arms, God will do with me what He wills." (Baunard, *Correspondence*, pp. 402–403)

In the days that followed, Frédéric wrote beautiful farewell verses to Amélie, which she placed at the base of a picture of angels done by Fra Angelico.

"Those angels were awaiting at the moment of departure from this earth the faithful who had been entrusted to their fostering care. You, my guardian angel, will remain on earth; your prayers will open Heaven to me. You will remain for yet a little while, to guide the footsteps of the darling child who was our joy. Teach her to think of me, endow her with your virtues. We shall meet again in the abode of love, and under the eyes of the good God Himself we shall love one another with a love that will know no end." (Baunard, *Correspondence*, p. 401)

In the first week of September 1853, when nearing death, Frédéric requested the sacraments of the dying. After administering them, the priest encouraged Frédéric to confide in the goodness of God. Without any fear Frédéric immediately replied, "'Why should I fear Him; . . . I love Him so'" (Baunard, *Correspondence*, p. 403). Lacordaire, his lifelong friend, later described Frédéric's deathbed calm as that "'which belonged neither to life nor to death'" (Baunard, *Correspondence*, p. 403). His serenity could be seen even in the features of his face.

Pause: How do you feel toward death? What gift do you hope to receive as you approach your own death?

Frédéric's Words

On 23 April 1853, Frédéric's last birthday on earth, he wrote his last will and testament at Pisa, Italy.

"In the name of the Father, Son and Holy Ghost. Amen.

"This day, the 23rd of April, 1853, on completing my 40th year, in great physical sickness but sound in mind, I express here in a few words my last wishes, intending to set them forth more fully when I shall have more strength.

"I commit my soul to Jesus Christ my Saviour, frightened at my sins, but trusting in His infinite mercy.

"I die in the Holy, Catholic, Apostolic, and Roman

Church. I have known the difficulties of belief of the present age, but my whole life has convinced me that there is neither rest for the mind nor peace for the heart save in the Church and in obedience to her authority.

"If I set any value on my research, it is that it gives me the right to entreat all whom I love, to remain faithful to the religion in which I found light and peace. My supreme prayer for my family, my wife, my child, and grandchildren, is that they will persevere in the Faith, despite any humiliation, scandals, or desertions which may come to their knowledge.

"I bid a farewell, short as the things of earth, to my dear Amélie, who has been the joy and the charm of my life, and whose tender care has softened all my pain for more than a year. I thank her, I bless her, I await her in Heaven. There, and only there, can I give her such love as she deserves.

"I give to my child the benediction of the patriarchs, in the Name of the Father and of the Son and of the Holy Ghost. I am sad that I cannot labour longer at the dear task of her education, but I entrust her absolutely to her virtuous and well-beloved mother." (Baunard, *Correspondence*, p. 386)

Reflection

As a Christian, Frédéric encountered the paradox of death: the certainty, the uncertainty; the sameness, the uniqueness; the end, the beginning. He had known death in his family with the demise of so many siblings. He had come to death's door himself several times throughout the years. Frédéric had been away from home when the news came that his father had stumbled and fallen in a tenement house and died shortly after. He was present at the bedside of his mother when her time had come. Indeed, Frédéric had voiced the hope that he would die like his mother.

Frédéric himself breathed his last on 8 September 1853, at approximately 7:50 p.m. He opened his eyes, raised his arms, and cried out: "'My God, my God, have mercy on me'" (Baunard, *Correspondence*, p. 403).

Christians die in faith. Faith enables Christians to affirm that death is not final—not the end of existence but the beginning of a new and eternal life. As one preface for Christian burial reads, "Lord, for your faithful people life is changed, not ended."

It is an ancient axiom that as we live so shall we die. The quality of our death will be similar to the quality of our life as we have lived it. Frédéric, in his younger days, had said, "'If religion teaches us how to live, it is to prepare us for death'" (Baunard, *Correspondence*, p. 82).

✧ Ponder Frédéric's words: "'Without [peace of heart] we may possess everything and yet not be happy; with it we can bear the hardest trials and the approach of death.'" Write a prayer to Frédéric asking for his intercession in obtaining for you this grace; tell him when and where you most need it.

✧ Reread Frédéric's last will and testament. Spend some time composing your own last will and testament. Remember to include in it the persons and the things that you love dearly in this life. Share this with someone who is important to you now, and put it in a place where it can be found at the time of your death.

✧ The words below appear on Frédéric's tomb in Paris. Do you think that they were appropriately selected for him?

> Many will praise his understanding;
>   it will never be blotted out.
> His memory will not disappear,
>   and his name will live through all generations.
> Nations will speak of his wisdom,
>   and the congregation will proclaim his praise.
> (Sirach 39:9–10)

What words would be appropriate for your tomb or the tomb of someone that you love? Read through the Book of Sirach if you need some ideas.

✧ Imagine yourself seriously sick and thinking that death may be close. What grace would you most like to receive? What prayer would you most want to pray? What words would you like to come from your lips as you breathed your last?

God's Word

"Do not let your hearts be troubled. Believe in God, believe also in me. In [God's] house there are many dwelling places. If it were not so, would I have told you that I go to prepare a place for you? And if I go and prepare a place for you, I will come again and will take you to myself, so that where I am, there you may be also. And you know the way to the place where I am going." Thomas said to him, "Lord, we do not know where you are going. How can we know the way?" Jesus said to him, "I am the way, and the truth, and the life." (John 14:1–6)

Closing prayer: Loving Creator, by his life and death Frédéric Ozanam offered you worship and praise. Renew in my heart the power of your love, so that neither death nor life may separate me from you.

H·O·S·A·N·N·A

✦ For Further Reading ✦

Baunard, Louis. *Ozanam in His Correspondence*. Trans. a member of the Council of Ireland, Society of Saint Vincent de Paul. Dublin, Ireland: Catholic Truth Society of Ireland, 1925.

Derum, James Patrick. *Apostle in a Top Hat: The Life of Frédéric Ozanam*. Saint Louis: Society of Saint Vincent de Paul, Council of the United States, 1995.

Des Rivières, Madeleine. *Ozanam*. Trans. James Parry. Montreal: Les Editions Bellarmin, 1989.

Dirvin, Joseph I., CM, trans. and ed., *Frédéric Ozanam: A Life in Letters*. Saint Louis: Society of Saint Vincent de Paul, Council of the United States, 1986.

Fagan, Austin. *Through the Eye of a Needle*. Middlegreen, England: Saint Paul Publications, 1989.

Schimberg, A. P. *The Great Friend: Frédéric Ozanam*. Milwaukee: Bruce Publishing Company, 1946.

Acknowledgments *(continued)*

The psalms in this book are from *Psalms Anew: In Inclusive Language,* compiled by Nancy Schreck and Maureen Leach (Winona, MN: Saint Mary's Press, 1986). Copyright © 1986 by Saint Mary's Press. All rights reserved.

All other scriptural quotations in this book are from the New Revised Standard Version of the Bible. Copyright © 1989 by the Division of Christian Education of the National Council of the Churches of Christ in the United States of America. All rights reserved.

The excerpts on pages 13, 21, 30, 31, 31, 32, 33, 44, 44, 44, 45, 49, 50, 50–51, 51, 52, 55, 56, 56–57, 62, 69, 69, 70, 74, 75, 75–76, 77, 77–78, 86, 87, 95, 102, 103, 107, 109, 113, 114, 114, 114, 114–115, 115–116, and 116 are from *Ozanam in His Correspondence,* by Louis Baunard, translated by a member of the Council of Ireland, Society of Saint Vincent de Paul (Dublin: Catholic Truth Society of Ireland, 1925), pages 410, 65, 3, 7, 137, 157, 63, 226, 201, 208, 402, 201, 10–11, 9–10, 304, 9, 343–344, 130, 258–259, 392, 98, 370, 400, 423, 89–90, 235–236, 423, 343, 65, 65, 273, 236–237, 97, 364, 402, 402–403, 401, 403, 403, 386, 403, and 82, respectively. Used by permission of Veritas Publications.

The excerpt by Pope John Paul II on page 14 is quoted in a letter by Amin A. de Tarrazi, international president of the Society of Saint Vincent de Paul.

The excerpts on pages 18, 37, and 61 are from *Ozanam,* by Madeleine des Rivières, translated by James Parry (Montreal: Les Editions Bellarmin, 1989), pages 29, 34, and 89, respectively. Copyright © 1989 by Les Editions Bellarmin.

The excerpts on pages 24–25, 37, 38, 64, 70–71, 74, 81, 87, 91–92, 93, 96, 97, 102, 102–103, 107, 108, 113, 113, and 113 are from *Frédéric Ozanam: His Life and Works,* by Kathleen O'Meara (New York: Christian Press Association Publishing Company, 1891), pages 147, 55, 103–104, 133, 186, 187, 248, 62 and 61, 63, 176–177, 335, 265, 275, 276, 344, 330, 333–334, 342, and 343, respectively.

The excerpts on pages 31, 32, 32, 36, 38–39, 42, 45, 47, 49–50, 61, 62, 63–64, 64, 75, 79, 80, 82, 94, 97, and 98 are from *Frédéric Ozanam: A Life in Letters,* translated and edited by Joseph I. Dirvin, CM (Saint Louis: Society of Saint Vincent de

Titles in the Companions for the Journey Series

Praying with Anthony of Padua
Praying with Benedict
Praying with Catherine McAuley
Praying with Catherine of Siena
Praying with Clare of Assisi
Praying with Dominic
Praying with Dorothy Day
Praying with Elizabeth Seton
Praying with Francis de Sales
Praying with Francis of Assisi
Praying with Frédéric Ozanam
Praying with Hildegard of Bingen
Praying with Ignatius of Loyola
Praying with John Baptist de La Salle
Praying with John Cardinal Newman
Praying with John of the Cross
Praying with Julian of Norwich
Praying with Louise de Marillac
Praying with Teresa of Ávila
Praying with Thérèse of Lisieux
Praying with Thomas Merton
Praying with Vincent de Paul

Order from your local religious bookstore or from

Saint Mary's Press
702 TERRACE HEIGHTS
WINONA MN 55987-1320
USA
1-800-533-8095